BASKETS OF SILVER

C. ROY ANGELL

BASKETS of SILVER

BROADMAN PRESS

NASHVILLE, TENNESSEE

Printed in the United States of America
3.5F61KSP

Contents

Baskets of Silver

A word fitly spoken is like apples of gold in pictures of silver.
—*Proverbs 25:11*

Dr. Bernard Taylor, who until his death taught Hebrew in the Eastern Baptist Seminary at Philadelphia, said that he preferred another translation of this beautiful text, "Apples of gold in pictures of silver." He read it like this: "Apples of gold in *baskets* of silver." Then he told us of the ancient royal custom in the Far East of placing on the banquet table as a centerpiece a silver filigree basket filled with golden apples. At some time during the meal, the basket was passed around, and every guest was invited to select one of the gleaming gold apples as a gift from the king. Dr. Taylor thought this was what Solomon had in mind when he wrote this particular sentence. He wanted the world to know that beautiful words can be as precious and as lovely as golden apples.

We, who live centuries after Solomon's time, have come to appreciate far more than the people of his day how true his words are. We live in a world of words. What we sometimes call a "cold war" is principally a war of words. Hitler averred that he would conquer more nations by the pen than by the sword. Not only did Hitler prove his theory, but we are frightened as we see it being proved by communism. We anxiously read our newspapers to find out, not so much what has been done in Asia, Europe, Africa and Central America, but what has been said. We realize afresh that words can wreck; words can revive; words can ruin; words can restore; and words can change our whole way of living.

This is true not only in international circles, but also in the little or the big homes in which we live. I remember hearing Dr. Ted Adams of Richmond tell about two young people who came to his office to arrange for their wedding.

He said, "I was talking to them about being kind to each other and closing each day on their knees to ask each other's and God's forgiveness for any unpleasant things that had been done or said during the day. I was stressing how important it is to be kind and considerate to each other when the young lady stopped listening to me and turned to her fiance. She put her hand over his and spoke with deep feeling. 'Remember that I said to you the other day that we should pledge never to speak an unkind word to each other?' She turned back to me and continued, 'My own home could have been a little bit of heaven. My father was wealthy, and we had a lovely house; but my mother and father quarreled with each other all the time, and in place of a little bit of heaven our home became a little corner of hell.' "

This young woman had realized that all of us should

keep close to our hearts that verse, "A word fitly spoken is like apples of gold in baskets of silver." Many of us could fill that silver basket full of different kinds of golden apples—words of praise, words of comfort, or words of encouragement. Let me take just three and enlarge upon them a little.

First, *humorous* or *happy* words are like golden apples. I hesitate to discuss this first lest someone think it isn't serious or religious enough, but in these days of tension and pressure, "A merry heart doeth good like a medicine."

A psychiatrist said recently, "Woe unto the man who loses his sense of humor. Laughter is the finest antidote for the acidity that eats ulcers in our stomachs. Will Rogers was doing the whole world good. Someone said of him after a short visit, 'It's just like being bathed in sunshine to be with Will Rogers. He has seen so many humorous, laughable, and happy things that a smile plays around his lips most of the time.' "

The Governor of one of our states tells this story: "I have one patrolman I wouldn't swap for any ten patrolmen that any other governor has—not because he is so good at being a policeman, but because he is like Will Rogers. When I get so swamped with the cares of the state, and he comes in off the road from 'way out yonder somewhere, and that genial face of his peeks into my office, and he says, 'Are you busy, Governor?' I say, 'No, come in here. If you've seen anything to laugh about, tell me, for I'm tired and loaded down, and I need to relax a minute.'

"He came in the other day and draped himself on the corner of my desk just like I was a fellow patrolman. With a smile on his face, he began to speak. 'Governor, I saw something funny. I was in Big Stone Gap, and there is a country store out there that is run by Mr. Jim, a fine Christian man. When I went in the other day, I saw a big sugar barrel half full of excelsior in the middle of the floor, and an old Dominique hen was setting in it.

" 'Mr. Jim, what's the idea?" I asked.

" 'Look under her, patrolman." I reached down and picked her up. Governor, there were two of the cutest little fuzzy white kittens that you ever saw. After I got over my astonishment, I asked him how it happened.

" 'Well," he said, "the old cat brought a kitten, carrying it by the nape of the neck, and dropped it right in the middle of the floor. She went back and brought another one and then looked at me as if to ask where she should put them. And so I put all three of them in the barrel. I needed them to keep the mice away. Then the old cat went out and was struck by a car on the highway. The old Dominique hen came in looking for a place to set. She finally decided to adopt the kittens, I reckon. It was a place to set, and there she is, anyhow." '

"The patrolman said, 'Just about that time a little towheaded boy came in—one suspender, freckled face, hair down over his eyes.

" 'Mr. Jim, what you got that old hen settin' in the middle of the barrel for?"

" 'Mr. Jim answered, "Look under her, son." The boy picked her up, and when he saw those two white kittens, he froze. He stood perfectly still, staring at the ceiling for half a minute, and then said, "Mister, I done et my last egg." ' "

Maybe all of us need the thing that Will Rogers and the patrolman had, the ability to see the humorous things in life, remember them, and pass them along to lighten burdens and release tensions in this pressure-bound world of ours. I don't think it irreverent to say that humorous words are "like apples of gold." I think, too, that a happy-hearted Christian, who can speak words that will chase the furrows out of the faces around him and leave a smile instead, will be pleasing the Master and fulfilling the Bible's admonition to "adorn the gospel."

Encouraging words, too, are "like apples of gold in baskets of silver." We use far too few of them. A word of encouragement, a word of appreciation, a little compliment can change a life. Immediately to our minds comes the message of Jesus to old heartbroken Simon Peter: "Go tell my disciples, and Peter, to meet me in Galilee." I am sure when those words came, Simon Peter was sitting apart from the others, and his chin was down on his chest. Of all men, he was the most miserable. He had failed his Master. He had denied him. I imagine he was thinking of what Jesus said: "No man, having put his hand to the plow, and looking back, is fit for the kingdom of God." Then came the messenger with two little words, "And Peter." You can see him spring up, mouth open, head bent forward, and you can hear him tell the messenger, "Say that again. Did he actually call my name? Does he still want me?" I am sure as they tramped that road down to the Sea of Galilee that Simon Peter marched out in front, head up, shoulders back. Two little words of encouragement changed his outlook on life.

Julian LeGrande, one of the richest merchants that Paris ever knew, hit on hard times during one of the great depressions in France. His big stores were in need of a hundred thousand dollars in cash. Julian went out to borrow it, but neither the banks nor his friends had any money. All day long he looked in vain, and he came back thinking, "Have I been in business for forty years, have I built up a chain of great stores, and now cannot even borrow a hundred thousand dollars, and the business may go under for the lack of this small sum, when we've taken in millions of dollars in a single year?" But there is more to this story.

Julian LeGrande said, "I was sitting in my office at sundown when a knock came on my door, and without lifting my head, I called, 'Come in.'

"The door opened, and a very striking, handsome man stood there. He was faultlessly attired, and he said, 'Julian LeGrande?'

"And I answered, 'Yes, sir, but you have the advantage of me.'

"He said, 'You probably would not know my name, but I'll tell you in a moment or two what it is. I understand that you need some money.'

" 'Yes, sir, I do.'

" 'How much do you need?'

" 'I need a hundred thousand dollars.'

" 'Well,' he said, 'if you will write your note for a hundred thousand dollars for a year with no interest, I'll give you my check for it. You can get the money from the bank tomorrow morning.' I got up slowly, my mouth hanging open, and I said, 'My friend, who in the world are you, and why do you do this?'

"He answered, 'Mr. LeGrande, my name is ———. I live in America now, but there was a time when I lived here, and I went to school here. You were Commissioner of Education, and you came to hear the final examination of our graduating class, and you helped give us our marks on our last speeches before the assembly. I was ragged, for I was of a very poor family. There were some rich boys, and I thought surely you would talk to some of them and commend them, but when I had finished, and the exercises were over, you came and laid your hand on my head and tilted it back so you could look into my face.

" 'You said, "Young man, you have something that the world needs. You can do better than you did today. It's in you. You can do better. You can do 'most anything you want to do if you set your heart on it. Now, make a man of yourself."

" 'You wouldn't remember those words, but every time I topped some achievement, and I'm very wealthy now, I've said, "Thank you, Mr. Julian LeGrande." And this day I have the pleasure of giving you a check for a hundred thousand dollars, just a tiny

interest payment on what you have meant to me.' "
"Apples of gold in baskets of silver"—words of encouragement.

> I shot an arrow into the air,
> It fell to earth, I knew not where.
> But long years after in the heart of an oak
> I found my arrow still unbroke.
>
> I breathed a song into the air
> It fell to earth, I knew not where.
> But long years after, in the heart of a friend,
> I found my song from beginning to end.

While we should never be thinking of the dividends that come to us from words of encouragement and appreciation, God thinks of them, and he who sees in secret rewards us openly. We can make life so much happier and so much finer for those around us if we will think to say the nice things and the cheery things to the people who need them. Where is the man who has not hugged some compliment to his heart and brought it out in the dark hours to let it light his way? Someone has said, "We will cross over a busy street just to pass and speak to someone who has said something nice about us, but we will walk around the block to miss coming face to face with someone who has criticized us."

Among the most beautiful golden apples are *words spoken for the Master*. Sometimes we think that the business of taking the words of salvation to people who are lost is the task of the minister and the Sunday school teacher, but Jesus never said it so. "Go ye into all the world," was his admonition. That word "ye" includes every Christian. It is not just a commission for the missionary, the evangelist, or the preacher. It is for every living soul of us who knows the message. Full many a time our sins of omission are bigger than our sins of commission. The words that we do not speak must bring heartache to our Heavenly Father.

One of the greatest soul-winners that I ever knew was a girl of seventeen who worked in a five-and-ten cent store. She was genuinely converted one Sunday morning and followed her Lord in baptism that same night. The next Sunday she walked down the aisle again, radiantly smiling, her arm slipped through the arm of another girl who worked in the same store. The two of them took their places in a Sunday school class where there were a number of girls who had never made a profession of faith. Seventeen times, in that first year of her Christian life, she came down the aisle with seventeen other girls.

Just at the end of that first year of glorious achievement, she was struck and killed by a car as she came along to church. When the hour for the funeral came, the church was banked with flowers, many of them from people who only knew her name and had seen her Sunday after Sunday as she led someone to make a profession of faith in Jesus. A long time before the funeral started there was no more standing room in the big auditorium. I have no way of knowing what words she used, but I do know they must have been "apples of gold in baskets of silver."

2

Rules of the Road

> *Enter ye in at the strait gate: for wide is the gate, and broad is the way, that leadeth to destruction, and many there be which go in thereat: Because strait is the gate, and narrow is the way, which leadeth unto life, and few there be that find it.*
>
> *—Matthew 7:13-14*

When Jesus said, "Narrow is the way, which leadeth unto life, and few there be that find it," He was not talking about eternity nor life hereafter, but life more abundant here on this good earth. Narrow is the way and strait is the gate that leads to the finest and the most glorious living this side of eternity.

The famous violinist, Fritz Kreisler, is a beautiful illustration of the truth of this passage. Recently I heard him play "Danny Boy" as an encore. It was one of those breath-taking experiences. As the last note died, two thousand people sprang to their feet, applauding, laughing, and crying. Every eye was fixed on the violinist, who stood with his head bowed. He, too, had been deeply moved by the music of his violin.

As he stood there, I remembered a thing that he had

said many years ago: "Narrow is the road that leads
to the life of a violinist. Hour after hour, day after
day, and week after week, for years, I lived with my
violin. There were so many things that I wanted to
do that I had to leave undone; there were so many
places I wanted to go that I had to miss if I was to
master the violin. The road that I traveled was a
narrow road and the way was hard." I am sure that
Kreisler had been reading this very passage and realized the truth of it. That moment when he stood
with bowed head and listened to the roar of applause
and saw the laughter and the tears in the vast au-
dience, he was enjoying abundant living.

This is what Christ is talking about. You can't
spread yourself out thin over a vast area and follow
every path that beckons and reach the high places in
life. Wasn't Christ thinking of the spiritual life and of
the discipline that was necessary to attain it? If we
follow the lines of least resistance, go with the crowd,
and forget our Christian obligations, we can easily
miss the heavenly places. There are many things that
we must leave undone, and there are certain things
that we must do if we would find what Jesus calls life.
These might be called "The Rules of the Road." Let
me mention three of them.

First, we will need to get and keep the main direction of life. Jesus talked a lot about *direction*. He very
seldom said, "Thou shalt" or "Thou shalt not," but
often he said in effect, "This do and thou shalt live,"
or "Follow me," or "This is the way."

One day one of his disciples asked, "Lord, how oft

shall my brother sin against me, and I forgive him? till seven times?" Quickly Jesus answered him, "Until seventy times seven." Of course, he didn't mean exactly 490 times. He was saying that the direction of your life should be toward forgiveness; he was saying that there is no limit to the number of times that we should forgive.

Another day, a man came to trap him and said, "Is it lawful to give tribute unto Caesar, or not?" I imagine the Master was smiling as he held out his hand and asked for a coin. You can see him turn it over and look at it as he spoke.

"Whose is this image?"

The answer was, "Caesar's." And I think he was still smiling when he handed it back and said, "Render therefore unto Caesar the things which are Caesar's; and unto God the things that are God's." In other words, the direction of your life should be toward giving.

In the Sermon on the Mount he said, "Ye have heard that it hath been said, Thou shalt love thy neighbor, and hate thine enemy, but I say unto you, Love your enemies." In other words, the direction of your life should be toward loving people.

On the night he instituted the Lord's Supper the disciples were quarreling among themselves about who should be the greatest among them. And so the Master girded himself with a towel and washed their feet. He said to them, "He that is greatest among you shall be your servant." We see again the direction of our lives should be toward serving. Another sentence im-

mediately comes to mind: "Inasmuch as ye have done
it unto one of the least of these my brethren, you have
done it unto me."

Some years ago a famous artist painted a rugged
picture. It was the picture of a pioneer wagon train
camped for the night. The covered wagons had been
drawn up in a circle. A campfire was in the center,
and the men were gathered around it. The leader of
the wagon train had a map spread on the ground in
the light of the campfire and was kneeling by it. He
had on a red flannel shirt. His beard was uncut; his
huge arms were exposed, sleeves rolled up; and his
shirt was open at the neck. On the map was a heavy
black line that zig-zagged halfway across the paper.
It marked the way they had come. The heavy black
line showed that they had veered north and south, but
the main direction was west. Evidently there had been
an argument about which way to go from here, but
the leader, with determination in his every feature,
placed his finger on the end of the black line, his other
arm pointed out toward the blue hazy mountains; and
he seemed to be saying, "We may have to go south
around a mountain or north to cross a river, but the
main direction we will keep is west."

The teachings of Jesus as well as his actions ought
to be the guide for shaping the main direction of our
lives. His whole life points away from hatreds and resentments and jealousies. Everything in it is gentle
and altogether lovely. He was forever telling us to be
careful about our thinking, for our thinking would
control the direction of our lives. "As he [a man]

thinketh in his heart so is he." "Lift up your eyes," Jesus is saying, "and take the long look. Where will you be twenty-five years from now if you keep on in the direction you are traveling?" Many of us have realized that the way we are living right this minute isn't good. Every time we examine ourselves closely we know there are some things we are doing which are not pleasing God, and most of us make up our minds that we are going to change our way of life. Tomorrow we are going to do differently. Someone has said, "The road to hell is paved with good intentions and good resolutions." God's statement is, "Now is the accepted time."

When we get the main direction of life, we should never be satisfied to live in the shallows, but in the words of Jesus, we should "*Launch out into the deep.*" It is so easy to follow the broad, level, smooth road. We let circumstances and people push us around. We live too much on the surface. Jesus, by example, "steadfastly set his face toward Jerusalem," overriding the protests of his friends and daring the defiance of enemies that he might accomplish the purpose for which he came.

The commencement speaker at Louisiana State University one year began his message with a story that deeply impressed me. It went something like this. "There was a wealthy father who had three sons. When the time came for him to leave this world, he sent for his sons to come and stand around his bed.

" 'I want to talk to you about my will,' he said. 'I am afraid you won't understand it unless I explain it to you. I have buried somewhere on the ranch a chest of gold and precious stones. There's a million dollars worth of gold and jewels in the iron chest. Now, when I die, the ranch goes to my oldest son for one year. If he finds that chest, then one half of the treasure and the ranch belong to him. The other half is to be divided between the other two sons. If at the end of the year he hasn't found it, then the second oldest son takes over, under the same conditions. And if at the end of the second year he hasn't found it, the third son takes charge in like manner. If none of you find it at the end of three years, then the whole thing goes to charity, and they will *know* where to find it.'

"The boys shifted from one foot to the other, and one of them said, 'Father, you want us to find it?'

"He said, 'I certainly do want you to find it.'

" 'Well, Father, if you want us to find it, won't you tell us how?'

"The father answered, 'I'll tell you exactly how to find it. Attend my words carefully, my sons. Plow deep, young men, plow deep.' The boys filed out.

"When the oldest son could get away from the other two, he slipped back to his father's room. 'Look Father, I am your oldest son. I am pretty sure you want me to have this ranch. Won't you tell me how to find it?'

" 'My son, kneel down and put your ear close to my lips, and I will tell you exactly how to find it.' The boy dropped down on his knees and turned his head, and the father whispered, 'My oldest son, *plow deep*, my son, *plow deep*.' The boy went out.

"The second son slipped in and in a hushed voice began, 'Father, you and I have always been pals. We have fished together and hunted together. If my oldest brother doesn't find it, won't you tell me how?'

"He answered, 'Yes, son, get down on your knees and put your ear close to my lips. *Plow deep*, son, *plow deep*.' The second son went out, and the third boy came in.

" 'Father, you don't want it to go to charity.'

" 'No, son, I don't.'

" 'Well, Dad, if the other two boys don't find it, tell me how.'

"He said, 'Son, get down on your knees and put your ear close to my lips. *Plow deep*, son, *plow deep*.'

"The oldest son took over. To his two brothers he said, 'I know where Father hid that chest. It's up in that deep ravine. I am going up there and turn that stream into the next ravine and turn over every rock in it. It's in that river bed somewhere.' So the oldest son spent the year. He didn't plow a furrow, and he didn't find the chest.

"Then the second son took over. He said, 'All right, brother, since you missed it, I know where it is. 'Way down yonder, ten miles down the ranch Father built that high tower. He had those beehives put around there. He didn't do it for nothing. He was protecting something. He spent a lot of time up in that tower, and he kept a watchman up there a great deal of the time. I am going down there and turn over that part of the ranch.' He spent a year; the weeds grew, and grass grew all over the big farm. The year was up, and he hadn't plowed a furrow, and he hadn't found the chest.

"The third son called together the servants. 'Come in here and get your plows and take these new plow points. They are longer than the ones you have been using. Hitch two teams to every plow in place of one. We are going to farm this land, for I have an idea that Father has buried this treasure in the subsoil and that he meant it when he said, *"Plow deep."* I am going to follow his directions.'

"His brothers protested, but the teams went out and turned the soil deep. One day, near noon, as the youngest son followed a deep-cutting plow, the point suddenly hit something hard, and the handles flew out of his hands. He dropped on his knees and frantically raked away the dirt. There was the top of the iron box, two inches down in the subsoil. Trembling from head to foot, he sat back on his heels and took off his hat. He turned his face to heaven and prayed, 'Father in heaven, I have learned my lesson, and I thank you for it. I will plow deep in everything that you want me to do in life. I won't take any short cuts. I won't leave anything undone that you want me to do. I will try to live a life as deep and true as Jesus did. I will be true to the finest that's in me and true to the finest that was in my father.' "

And so I would say the second rule of the road is *plow deep*. Isn't this what Jesus was talking about when he said, "The children of this world are in their generation wiser than the children of light?" He was not condoning the steward who stole from his master in

order that he might have security for the future, but
he was comparing the ingenuity of men in the com-
mercial world to the ingenuity of Christians. He was
telling us that they left no stones unturned. They always plowed deep when profits were at stake. He was
censuring Christians for surface living and for shal-
lowness. He would have us do God's work with everything that's in us. When he said, "Thou shalt love the
Lord thy God with all thy heart, and with all thy
soul, and with all thy mind, and with all thy strength,"
he was challenging us to use everything that we have
in the kingdom work. This was just another way of
saying, *Plow deep.*

A third rule for us to remember is that God needs
human hands to do his work. Full many a time God
answers prayer by finding a third person who can
supply the help that is needed.

This thought was beautifully expressed in an incident that happened in a little village in France after
the war. A detachment of soldiers had been left as
occupational troops to keep order in the town. Time
hung heavy on their hands. One day they decided to
help the villagers restore their bombed homes and
city. They started on the church. It was a big job,
for the church had received a direct hit. They worked
joyously and cheerfully, cleaning up debris, putting
back the windows, and rebuilding the pews. Amid the
debris they found a marble statue of Christ. It was
badly broken, but they managed to cement it together
and set it up in its niche in the wall. But search as they
would, they could not find the hands for the statue of

Christ. And so when they had finished arranging the statue in its place, a moment of inspiration came to one of them. He made a placard and hung it on the statue. These simple words were printed on it, "He has no hands but yours."

3

Who Crucified Christ?

. . . smitten of God.

—Isaiah 53:4

I have a very dear Jewish friend who is a merchant in a large city. One day as I sat on the counter in his big store and talked religion, he said, "Dr. Angell, there's one question that I've been wanting to ask you a long time, but I have been afraid it would offend you. Would you promise not to get angry with me if I ask you a question about your Christ?"

I said, "Why, certainly, I won't get angry with you. I'll be delighted to try to answer any question that you can ask about my Christ."

My friend said, "Dr. Angell, is a part of the prejudice against my people a result of the fact that they killed your Christ?"

I'm sure my mouth and eyes were both wide open as I answered. "Why, no indeed. I've never even thought of it. Personally, it has never crossed my mind that you killed my Christ. After all, he was yours; he was one of your nationality, in the first place, and in the second place, you didn't kill him. Turn and read

20

the fifty-third chapter of Isaiah, and you will clearly see that your people did not kill Jesus."

Immediately my mind went back to a most impressive message delivered by President G. Earl Guinn, of Louisiana College. I am deeply indebted to him for the rest of this message. In fact, I do not know how much of it is his and how much of it is mine.

Who did crucify Christ? Who did put him to death?

It would not be fair for us to try to answer that question without beginning with the *historical facts*. Practically all the historical facts that we have come from four men, Matthew, Mark, Luke and John. We have one little paragraph from Josephus. We have some philosophical rumblings from Philo; but four men give us all the data that we have. Mark, who wrote first, tells us just the bare, straight facts—that the Roman soldiers put Jesus to death at the command of Pontius Pilate. Luke goes behind the scene a little and tells us that pressures were brought to bear on Pontius Pilate which caused him to make the command. John weaves a very graphic, though not a beautiful, picture. Matthew, Mark, Luke, and John give the facts—just the facts—with a little of the background and the pressure. The Romans nailed him to the cross; they ran a spear into his side. The Roman soldiers put him to death. Historically, Jesus was crucified by Pontius Pilate and the Romans.

Now, look at the theological point of view. Who put Jesus to death? There is a sense in which God put Jesus to death. Read the fifty-third chapter of Isaiah, and you'll find that Jesus was "smitten of God and afflicted." Did God put Jesus to death? Beloved, I am perfectly sure that God was not surprised at all at what happened on Calvary. You can turn back to the Old Testament and read another story that gives a partial picture of it. One day Abraham called his son Isaac and took him up Mount Moriah, built a stone altar, put him on it, tied his hands and feet, took out the knife, and lifted it up to make a sacrifice out of Isaac. But a voice from heaven stopped him; the knife never descended. When Jesus Christ was stretched out on the cross on Calvary, and a nail was placed in the palm of his hand, and a hammer was raised to drive it in, there was no voice; God did not speak.

God could have stopped it. Nor did God stop that Roman soldier when he drew his spear and pierced the side of Jesus. The heavens were silent. God did not interfere. Read John 3:16 very slowly: "For God so loved the world, that he gave his only be-gotten Son. . . ." Read it. Here is one of the most gloriously distinctive tenets of Christianity. Herein Christianity differs from every other religion of the world. From the beginning of time men have been conscious that they have sinned and displeased God. They have offered blood sacrifices to right themselves with God. They have offered everything in their pos-session to appease the wrath of their gods. They have felt, without exception, that they must bring a sacrifice and put it on the altar. *In Christianity, God, not man, furnishes the sacrifice.* "God so loved the world that he *gave* his only begotten Son." Through Jesus God fur-nished an atonement for our sins. Here, then, is shouting ground. And so, in a very beautiful and glorious sense, God is responsible for the death of Jesus.

Let us ask the question again. This time we ask it of the Master himself. "Jesus, who put you to death on Calvary?" And what would he answer?

He would answer, "Nobody did it. Nobody did it. I did it." He would say, "Don't you remember I told you that no man taketh my life from me? I have power to lay it down, and I have power to take it up.

"Don't you remember when Pontius Pilate said to me, 'You don't answer me. Don't you know I have power to put you to death?' And I said to Pontius Pilate, 'You have no power, except that which God gives to you. You are just a puppet.'

"Don't you remember when Simon Peter jerked out his sword and stood between me and that Roman soldier? I laid my arm around his shoulder, and I said, 'Simon, put your sword up. Don't you know I can call down seventy-two thousand angels to protect me, if I want to?' No man put me to death. I had the power to stay alive or to lay down my life as an atonement for sin, as a revelation of God's love for the world. *I* did it. *I* did it."

Did the devil have anything to do with it? Who was it that put it into the heart of Judas Iscariot to be the treacherous betrayer of Jesus? The devil did it. Who else but the devil could have put it into the Roman soldier's mind to go out and get enough thorns to make a crown and put it on Jesus Christ's head? Only Satan could have thought of it. Who would have ever put it into their minds to spit on him and put a rod in his hand, mock him and ridicule him? Ah, beloved, Satan had a hand in it. Who put Jesus to death? Roman soldiers? God? Satan? Or as Jesus said, "Nobody?"

But there is another answer to that question, "Who put Jesus to death?" *We did it. We did it.* We did it because Jesus died for our iniquities, our transgressions, and our sins. Sin drove the nails. The very same transgressions and iniquities and sins which were present in that crowd of people who stood around the cross on Golgotha that day are present in every assembly of people today.

Let us take the first sin. I think it was avarice, greed, and covetousness, all tied up in one bundle labeled Sadducees. The Sadducees had charge of the Temple. They had charge of the Temple by virtue of the fact that they named and selected the high priest. Whoever named and selected the high priest ruled the Temple. Jesus went in his early ministry and looked at his Father's house, the Temple, and what he saw made him very angry. He drove out the money-changers who bought and sold, and then he went back just before his death, and once more he became angry and turned the tables over. He knotted a cord and drove out every one of the money-changers and all those who bought and sold and he said, "My [Father's] house is the house of prayer: but ye have made it a den of thieves." That made the Sadducees furious. They were angry, not because they had any quarrel with the religion of Jesus Christ, for they didn't have enough religion to quarrel about, but because Jesus was hurting their pocketbooks.

The way they made their money was, in modern language, "a racket." People from everywhere drove their bullocks and sheep and goats up the roads that led to Jerusalem in order to make an offering. The money-changers met them and smilingly said, "The long journey has been too hard on your offering, and it is blemished. You remember what Moses said, 'The offering must be perfect,' but don't feel too bad, for we can help you out. We will give you a perfect offering for this blemished one of yours, and it will cost only a little extra money." Then, of course, they took this animal and exchanged it with someone else. Like-wise, the Roman coins were used throughout the realm, but Roman coins were not acceptable in the Temple, and so the money-changers smilingly said, "We'll take your Roman coins and give you Hebrew money in exchange, and the exchange will not cost you much extra."

Jesus broke up their racket, and as they stood out-side the Temple, I am sure they vowed vengeance upon the Christ. Thus greed and materialism and avarice drove the nails into the hands of Jesus.

Of course, we don't have anything like that today! There isn't any materialism, there isn't any greed, there isn't any avarice, there isn't any covetousness, there isn't anybody in this beautiful land of ours who would ever let a few thousand dollars come between them and Jesus. *Of course there is!* And of course, ma-terialism and the very same sins and the very same power that the Sadducees had and used to put pressure on Pontius Pilate and on everybody that had anything to do with the crucifixion of Jesus is right here today. Who crucified him? We did. With the very same sins over and over and over again we crucify Jesus Christ. When we do the thing that's wrong for the sake of a few dollars, we drive a nail into his hands. We crucified him. We did it.

Another of the sins is cowardice. Pontius Pilate wanted to turn Jesus loose. He wanted to turn him loose, but he was afraid. It's stated in plain language. He was afraid. Do we have any cowardice today? I wonder how many people there are who have never opened their mouths to speak to someone else about Jesus Christ because they were cowards? I wonder how much of that cowardice is in our pulpits today? I wonder how fearlessly the pulpit affirms today that if we do not tithe we are thieves and robbers? This is according to God's Word. God says that if you do not tithe you are a thief. "Will a man rob God?," he asks. The Bible says that a man who doesn't pay his tithe robs God. I wonder how firmly we say that? And with how much fearlessness do we say it in the pulpits of this country today? I wonder if the cowardice that crucified Jesus Christ starts in the pulpits? I wonder, too, if it doesn't extend to all of us? I wonder how many young people refuse to stand up and be counted for Jesus Christ because they are afraid they'll lose some popularity? Cowardice had a big part in making Jesus carry a cross up Calvary that day.

Another sin was walking the streets of Jerusalem

that day—the sin of *the wrong choice*. Pilate said to the people milling below him, "It's the custom on this particular day to release to you a prisoner. Shall I release Jesus Christ?" And I imagine Pilate was smiling as he added, "Or shall I release Barabbas?" Barabbas was a *Roman* prisoner. Jesus Christ was a Jewish prisoner. Do you know why Barabbas was in prison? He had led a rebellion that tried to overthrow the Roman rule. He tried to set the Jewish people free. He had much in common with the Maccabees. Now, here is a startling parallel. Barabbas means *"son of the father."* Jesus likewise identified himself as *"Son of the Father,"* same title, but not the same meaning. And Barabbas' first name was Jesus, too. So Pilate said, "Well, all right, here's Barabbas, who is in prison because he tried to set you *free from the Roman rule.* Here's Jesus Christ, who is a prisoner today because he came, as he said himself, *to set you free,* and 'if the Son of Man shall make you free, you shall be free indeed,' were his own words. Which one of them do you want to go free? Which one of them do you want to die? Which one? I'll crucify one of them and turn the other one loose." In other words, Pilate said, "Choose between *material freedom* on one side and *spiritual freedom* on the other side." And they chose material freedom.

They said, "Turn Barabbas loose. Crucify Jesus." I wonder if that is ever done today? I wonder if people ever choose this day materialism and crucify Jesus? I wonder if a man ever says, "I want to be free and live as I please, like the prodigal son said, without any restraint. I want to live my own life. It's my life, and

I'm going to live it just like I please." Do we choose that instead of the abundant life Jesus gives?

As I look back at this whole picture, there seems to be just one thing for us to do, and that is to get down on our knees and thank God for his love and his mercy and his forgiveness and for the Christ who left the ivory palaces and came to be the atonement for our sins. Then I think we will want to rededicate our lives and ask God to help us never to drive another nail into the hands of Christ.

4

In a Far Country

> ". . . and took his journey into a
> far country."
>
> —Luke 15:13

Lindsay A. Glegg, the English author and speaker, tells a most interesting experience about the story of the prodigal son. He relates it thus: "I was taking a long train trip and needed something to read. On the newsstand I saw a small volume entitled, *The World's Best Stories*. I love good stories; so I bought the volume. Comfortably seated in the train, I looked down the table of contents. I was startled to read the title of the fourth story, 'The Prodigal Son,' by Jesus. I am a preacher, and I smiled with deep satisfaction. To myself I said, 'The man who gathered this collection must have been a genius. He must have eyes that see and ears that hear, to know that the story of the prodigal son ranks among the best stories ever written.' I decided on an experiment. I would start with the first story in the book and read straight through the one on the prodigal son. I determined to be fair-minded about it and an impartial judge. I wanted to know whether I was just prejudiced or whether it deserved to rank among the best. It took me a couple of hours to read the ones in front of it; then I turned with delight to 'The Prodigal Son.' Before I had finished reading it, the tears were streaming down my face, and when I came to the end, I said a reverent, 'Amen. It's the best story in the world.' "

We all know that Jesus usually told the parables to illustrate some statement or message that he was anxious to drive home. This story was no exception. A part of it was meant for those scribes and Pharisees who were nudging each other and with turned up noses were saying, "He eats with sinners." He was saying to them indirectly, what he later said directly: "The Son of Man came to seek and save sinners." Someone recently said that if Jesus had found the scribes and Pharisees diligently and earnestly trying to lead sinners to God he could have made this story even more beautiful. He could have told a part of it like this, I think:

One day that elder son came in and asked the father and mother to sit down with him in the living room, for he had something important to discuss with them. When they were comfortably seated he said, "Mother, I heard you sobbing last night in the night. I know you're miserable because my younger brother is way out yonder somewhere, and we don't know where he is. The other night I came in sort of late, and I noticed a light in my brother's room. I drove the spurs into my horse as I turned into the gate, and I flew up to his room. I thought he was home. I was just going to hug him and tell him I was so glad that he was back, for life has been terrible around here without him. I sat down on his bed and cried to myself for half an hour. Mother, how long have you been keeping a light burning in his room?"

Then he turned to his father, "Dad, I saw you the other day. You and I don't talk about him much, but I saw you when you climbed up that highest hill out there where you could see down that winding road. You sat up there all afternoon. You were watching for him. I plowed on, but the tears plowed some furrows down the dust on my cheeks. I washed my face before I came in to supper. Now, let's face it. We're miserable; all of us are. Let me go find that boy. I can find him. I can find him and bring him home."

The mother said, "No, no, no, you can't go. We've lost one boy, and we can't possibly spare you."

And his dad reached over and patted his shoulder and said, "Son, you're a noble boy, but we can't let you go."

And then the boy got up and walked around, "Look, it's just like a funeral here all the time. I miss him just as much as you do. I put on a laugh and a brazen front and joke some, but I'm crying inside. I've got to go find my brother." The next morning he started. That father and mother walked with him a long way and watched him as long as they could see him.

One day that father sitting on the same hill saw two boys coming up that dusty road. He couldn't get there fast enough. He called to the servants as he ran past the house, "Bring a robe. Bring some sandals. Bring a ring." And I'm sure he went to that youngest brother first and smothered his repentant talk against his shoulder and put the robe on him.

Then, with quiet respect, he turned to that older son, reached out and took hold of his shoulders, and whispered, "All that I have is thine, for ever and ever. You're the grandest son I ever knew."

But the older son pushed him off gently and said, "No, Father, I told my brother if he would come home we'd just forget all about that other division of the property, and we would be just the same two brothers we always were."

Then the old father said to the servants, "Go kill not just one of those fatted calves, but go kill two of them. Call the neighbors together. The seat of honor at the table belongs to the elder son tonight. He's the hero of this occasion."

Beloved, I think that's the way Jesus would liked to have told that story if he had not had to give the religious leaders of his time a rebuke. No, if he had not had to give the religious leaders of *all* times a rebuke, he might have told it that way. You and I haven't done much better than they did. We haven't gone into that far country and found a boy that had gone astray and brought him back—not half often enough.

Three questions come up naturally when we try to see the message that Jesus put in this story for us.

Where is that far country? The best answer that I have ever seen was the one that Dr. Ellis Fuller gave. "It is anywhere that a man tries to live without God." It can be the most beautiful city in America; it can be the most beautiful home in your city. I used to think of the far country in the words of Kipling, "Where the trails run out and stop." I used to think it was some wild western frontier town where the mud or dust was deep in the streets, where there was no paint on the houses, where the outlaws lived, and men killed each other for nothing. I used to think it was this town in nowhere that was filled with the scum of the earth, where saloons and bawdy houses were the only hangouts men had, but alas, I realize that a man can be in a far country in the house that is next to mine, where the church bells peal out every Sunday. But the far country is just as Dr. Fuller said, anywhere, anywhere that a man tries to live without God.

Why do people go into that far country? Sometimes they go for the same reason that this young man went—to find what they call *freedom* to do as they please. They don't want to be restrained by the Spirit of Jesus. Their philosophy of life is expressed in their own words, "My life is my own, and I will live it as I please." Maybe they do not say it in such bold words, but their actions speak all too plainly.

There came into my office one day a young lawyer with as fine a personality as I have ever seen. He was a most successful superintendent of a department in our Sunday school and was fast becoming a prominent attorney. He sat down on the chair farthest from my desk. He leaned over and buried his face in his hands for a while. Finally, he raised up and, with a miserable countenance, said, "Doctor, I have to resign as superintendent of my department."

Astonished, I asked him what in the world had happened.

He answered "Nothing has happened, and I haven't done anything disgraceful, but I have to resign. I can't tell you why. I have put this conference off for nearly a month because I dreaded to face you and say what I am saying. Please don't ask me any questions. I can't answer them, but I have to resign." That day he left my office and walked straight into a far country, for he was going to accept a position that would be inconsistent with his activity in the kingdom of God. Through the years that have followed he has never returned from that far country.

Sometimes they go to a far country because of *resentments*. Not long ago a father called to ask me to visit him and his wife. They have one of the most beautiful homes I have ever seen. It must have cost a hundred thousand dollars. After we had talked a few minutes, he pulled his chair up a little closer to mine and said, "I am anxious about my boy. Neither he nor any of his family go to Sunday school and church any more, and I think a visit from you might help a little. My wife and I both worry and grieve about them continually. Please help me with them."

I promised him I would, and then after a while I gently asked, "Why don't you and your wife come to our church any more?"

He answered without a moment's hesitation, "There is one man in your church that I deeply resent, and I can't be happy nor comfortable in the same church with him. I can't take the Lord's Supper with him.

I can't worship where he is." I didn't have the heart to tell him that his resentments had sent him into a far country and had carried his family with him, and further, that two darling little children were born into a home that was built in the middle of a far country.

Is there any way for a man to get back from the far country? There is much truth in that Chinese proverb, "There is no road back."

Omar Khayyam expressed it in an unforgettable way:

> The Moving Finger writes;
> And having writ,
> Moves on;
> Nor all your Piety nor wit shall lure it back,
> To cancel half a line,
> Nor all your Tears wash out a word of it.

A sports writer for a New York paper was deeply impressed by this truth one day as he watched a baseball game. In typical sports jargon he said, "Lou Gehrig came to bat with two out in the ninth inning. The winning runs were on second and third. New York was one run behind and the hit meant a win. The count on Lou Gehrig went to three balls and two strikes. The grandstand was in an uproar. The pitcher wound up deliberately and the third strike came smoking in straight over the middle of the plate and the umpire called "Strike three," for Lou Gehrig hadn't moved his bat. Very slowly Lou turned and spoke to the umpire. At this the crowd went wild, for no one had ever heard Lou Gehrig argue with an umpire. We reporters all piled over the seats and right out onto the field. We swarmed around the umpire. "What did Lou Gehrig say to you?" we all asked in one breath. "Whatever it was would make headlines on the sport page."

The umpire smiled and yelled to Lou Gehrig to come over. "Lou," he said, "tell the boys what you said to me when I called that third strike on you."

Lou looked a little bewildered as he answered, "Mister Ump, I only said, 'I would give ten dollars to have that one back.'"

The reporter was so impressed that when he wrote up the story, he added, "There are people all over the world who would give ten dollars or ten thousand dollars to get just one minute back and for the privilege of changing something they said or did in that minute." But there is no road back.

In a very deep sense there was no road back for the prodigal son. To be sure, he came back, but *not like he went out.* Here is one of the most glorious messages of Christianity. While we cannot change the past nor get it back to cancel one regrettable thing, God can blot out all the yesterdays from his book of remembrance, and we can have a clean page and start life new. God has promised to bury our sins as deep as the sea and separate us from them as far as the east is from the west, for the blood of Jesus cleanses from all sins. This is one of the great truths that Jesus presented in this beautiful parable. The welcome home by the father, who represented God, was deep and sincere.

Let me illustrate. Len Broughton tells of the most disturbing thing that ever happened to him in a revival service. In substance he said, "The church in which I was preaching had a paid quartet that led the music. While we were singing the invitation hymn one night, a lady whose face reflected a sinful life, walked down the aisle. The pastor, who was standing by me, whispered, 'She was once a member of the quartet in our choir until she went away from God and from all of her friends.'

"The thing that disturbed me was that suddenly nobody was leading the music, and I looked around and saw that the quartet had walked out. And I thought, 'How in the world can a woman ever come back and join the church when the group she sang with deliberately stopped singing and went out the back door.' But I was mistaken, for then the side door opened and the four singers came in. They knelt around her and sat by her; they hugged her; they cried with her; they prayed for her. When the service was over, the five of them went out together to another room and finished their conference." Yes, full many a time the way is made easier by somebody who cares— a mother's prayers, a brother's pleading, a father's invitation, or searching friends. Full many a time the story reads as I think Jesus would have liked to have told it. Yes, there is a way back—the same way back that the prodigal found, the way of repentance and confession.

5

The Cross Pull

*For the good that I would I do not:
but the evil which I would not, that I
do.*

—Romans 7:19

The words *cross pull* are not mine. They belong to an internationally famous radio commentator. He was a guest in our city, and I had the privilege of eating lunch with him and some eight or nine businessmen. After the meal was over and he had discovered that I was a minister, he said, "Just a minute, Doctor, I want to tell you a story, rather, an incident from my own life.

"Years ago when I was just a young fellow, I was on a ranch in the West—a guest for a few days. There was one little bandy-legged cowboy on that ranch that was about the most heart-broken, miserable man I ever saw. He had raised—rather, he had reared—a colt, and it had grown to be a big, fine stallion. He and that horse loved each other very much. Everybody teased the little cowboy about his horse. It would follow him around like a dog. The horse had stepped in a gopher hole and sprained his ankle and had been put out in the big pasture. Some wild horses had broken in and then broken out again, and the favorite had gone with them. The cowboy was just miserable.

"The second evening I was on the ranch, one of the other hands raced into the ranch yard as hard as his horse could run, yelling to the dejected little cowboy at the top of his voice, 'Found your horse! Found your horse! He's with a herd of wild horses not far from here, down in the canyon.'

"It was late in the evening, and so the little cowboy got set to go after him before daylight the next morning. I persuaded him to let me go along. We got up on top of the rimrock so we could look down the long canyon and decide how best to stalk his horse. We could see the horses grazing quietly. I lay up on the rimrock on my stomach and watched as the little cowboy went down on foot. He did a beautiful piece of stalking until he was close enough for his voice to reach his horse. I saw him stand up, and I saw all of those horses suddenly on the alert, their heads up. I knew he was talking to his horse for all he was worth. Then the herd bolted—all but one. One of them stood still, but he didn't know what to do. He looked at the other horses, and he took a step or two; then he looked back at the cowboy, pranced around a little, then looked again.

"I could feel—I could almost see the cross pull in that fine stallion. It must have been terrible. There was the master whom he had loved and there was the wild herd with which he had run. Which way should he go? I thought for a moment the cowboy had lost, for the horse took half a dozen steps as if to catch up with the herd, galloping away in a cloud of dust. Then he stopped and looked back, and with his head up and neck arched, he trotted to his master. The cowboy put a rope around his neck, patted and caressed him, and cried a little, too, I found out later. I could see the horse nuzzling his pockets, and the cowboy reached into one of them and brought out a hand full of lump sugar."

I was listening intently to the story when the well-known commentator looked straight into my face and said, "Doctor, I just laid my head down on my hands up on the rimrock and prayed, 'Dear Lord, if ever I am tempted to run with the wild crowd in life, O Lord, let me listen to my Master's voice; let me come back to him.' That was my prayer then, and that's been my prayer ever since."

Now, beloved, that's a sermon in itself, not preached by a preacher, but by a radio commentator. That's exactly what Paul is saying. "There's a tug of war going on inside of me, a cross pull. The things I would not do I do. The things I don't want to do, those are the things I do. There's a cross pull inside of me." That is a situation that finds every one of us many times during our lives.

You may have read the lines an English Tommy is supposed to have written during World War I.

> The padre 'e says I'm a sinner,
> John Bull 'e says I'm a saint,
> Both of 'em bound to be liars
> I'm neither of them, I ain't.

> I'm a man, and a man is a mixture
> Right down from the day of his birth
> Where a part of 'im come from Heaven
> And a part of 'im come from earth.

Look at four places where this cross pull with its tension strikes most often.

The first place is what Paul is talking about when he speaks of *the cross pull between that which is right and that which is wrong.* The Bible has a fearful word for it —*temptation.* It hounds us from childhood to the end of life. I think Paul was referring to this when he said, "The time of my departure is at hand. I have fought a good fight." At least a part of that fight was inside of him. We might well paraphrase those lines and let them read:

> The greatest battles that ever were fought
> Shall I tell you where, and when?
> They were not fought on battlefields
> They were fought *inside of men.*

I'd finished speaking on a subject akin to this at Ridgecrest one summer, and after the service was over a dear little white-haired lady came up and with eyes shining said, "Doctor, do you have a deacon by the name of Bob ———?"

And I said, "Yes, ma'am, I certainly do. Are you acquainted with him?"

She said, "I taught him in day school. When he first came into my class in the school back in the mountains in Tennessee, I had a pretty rough class, and I knew I was going to have trouble with discipline. I sort of built my hopes on him because he had such a good, honest face, and when I talked to him he seemed to be so solid and well grounded in the things that were right. Maybe he could keep the others in line; maybe he would be the leader I needed. I fervently hoped he would measure up to my expectations.

"And then one day they all did something that was pretty bad, and Bob was in the crowd. I was so disappointed, and I had to discipline him. I met him a few days later on the playground and I said, 'Bob, I was disappointed in you. I didn't think you were going to run with them and let them take you where you ought not to have gone. I counted on you for finer things than that.'

"He looked down at his toes and dug them in the dust and said, 'Miss Thorpe, I was surprised and disappointed in myself. I never intended to do that.' And then a few moments later he looked up, and his eyes were bright.

" 'Miss Thorpe, as long as you live, I'll never let you down again. You can count on me from now on. I'll never let you down.'

"I said to him, 'Now, that's the boy I thought you were.'

" 'Miss Thorpe, they called me a coward; they called me a sissy; they said I was afraid. But they won't get away with that any more.'

"He kept that promise beautifully. He was deacon material before he was grown."

Yes, that old cross pull between what's right and what's wrong is ever with us. How often we come in contact with it in our own lives. What a glorious thing it is when we can say to God, "I'll never let you down any more" and then hear God say, "This is my beloved son in whom I am well pleased."

Many times this cross pull develops between our *feelings* and *instincts* on one side and God's Word on the other side. You remember that verse in Proverbs which reads, "There is a way that seemeth right to man, but the end thereof are the ways of death." Isn't God saying that you cannot trust your instincts and your feelings always? Isn't he saying that some things that seem right to us may be entirely wrong and that it is a dangerous thing to follow our feelings and wishes and desires? They have a way of glossing over the facts. They tempt us to rationalize and excuse our actions. I think the best illustration that I have ever found for this verse of Scripture was given me by that fine young preacher, Forrest Lanier, of Rome, Georgia.

He said, "I was a pilot in the Second World War and received my training at Kelly Field, San Antonio. The first time I climbed into the cockpit of a plane and looked at the bewildering instrument board, the instructor gave me a real shock. Very slowly he pointed out the uses of each instrument.

" 'Here is your compass,' he said. 'You will need it all the time, for direction is most important. Here's your altimeter. It will tell you how high you are above the ground. Here is another instrument that will tell you when your plane is level with the horizon.' After completing the explanation of everything on the panel he said, 'Now, listen to me carefully. *You will have to trust this instrument board implicitly or it will kill you.*'

"I guess my astonishment showed on my face. 'Kill me?' I said.

"He repeated with emphasis, 'Kill you!'

" 'Kill me?' I said. 'How?'

"He said very slowly, 'The time will come when you will feel that you are going in the right direction, but you must not trust that feeling. You must trust this compass. If you dare trust your feelings you are going to get killed. Some night in the dark you are going to get the feeling that your plane is not level, but you mustn't dare to try to level it by your feelings. Look at your instrument board. You've got to learn to trust these instruments, fly by them, be guided by them, and forget your feelings."

Forrest stopped talking to me for a little while, and I asked, "Did it ever happen?"

A bit of a smile played over his face as he answered. "I'm ashamed to tell you. I was alone in a storm in the middle of the night, and I was being tossed around until every strap on my harness was creaking. I had a feeling that my right wing was too low, and so I pulled it up. It still seemed too low, and I pulled it up some more. By and by I thought my shoulder straps were too tight. I made up my mind I was going to loosen them as soon as I got a chance. Then suddenly I came to myself and looked at the instrument board. I was upside down and going in the wrong direction. The cold perspiration stood out all over me, and the words of the instructor came ringing in my ear, 'Fly by your instrument board; trust it and not your feelings.' "

And then he quoted this verse to me, "There is a

way that seemeth right to man, but the end thereof is death. "

Full many a time there is a cross pull between the way God tells us to walk and the way our instincts or urges or feelings dictate.

And then oftentimes there is a cross pull between the *good* and the *best*. As has been so well said, "The good is often the enemy of the best." It is so very easy to be satisfied with the good, but that isn't what Jesus asks of us. His question in the Sermon on the Mount was, "What do ye more than others?" And like unto it, "Except your righteousness shall *exceed* the righteousness of the scribes and the Pharisees, ye shall in no case enter into the kingdom of heaven." More than thirty years ago, Dr. A. C. Dixon prayed a prayer with just one sentence in it. I'm sure he made it brief purposely. He wanted the group of ministers who were gathered around him to keep in mind a mighty truth. I don't believe one of us has ever forgotten that prayer. This was the sentence: "Lord, help us not to fill our lives up with things that are good [he paused for half a minute before finishing the prayer] to the exclusion, dear Lord, of the things that are best."

Dean Brown of Yale was thinking of this same tug of war when he wrote that paragraph about young Americans in the city of Rome. In substance he said, "I was staying at the same hotel in Rome with a group of young Americans. They were a wholesome, happy crowd. I never saw them do anything that would make me ashamed of my fellow countrymen except this. Every morning I found them gathered around the swimming pool or just loitering around the hotel lobby. Every evening when I returned from seeing the wonders of Rome, I found them still loafing and idling.

"By and by I became furious, and while I didn't say it to them, I said it aloud, 'What right have such people in Rome anyhow? What right have they any-where—people with the opportunity of seeing mar-velous paintings, architecture, and historical places, wasting their time and filling up the day with trivial things, when they might have enriched their lives by communing with the best?' "

Last, there is that cross pull between *selfishness* and *service*. Remember when James and John came to Jesus? Matthew said their mother came, too, and she said to the Master, "Grant that these my two sons may sit, the one on thy right hand and the other on thy left, in thy kingdom."

Jesus answered, "To sit on my right hand or on my left hand is not mine to give." What did he mean? Wasn't he all powerful? Couldn't he let one of them sit on one side and one on the other if he wished? He made it plain a little later when they were discussing and arguing about who was the greatest in the king-dom. They were in the upper room after the Lord's Supper was over when Jesus said to them, "But he that is greatest among you, let him be as the younger; and he that is chief, as he that doth serve." These positions of greatness are not given away; they are to be earned. They are to be earned by the people who beautifully and in a joyous way serve the best.

When William Taft was elected President of the

United States, a friend of his boyhood days came immediately to see him. She had married a house painter and she came to ask a favor.

"I want you to make my husband Secretary of Commerce of the United States."

He smiled genially, and trying not to offend her, he said, "You know I must have a big man for that place. I need a big man, a man who has had experience and is well known."

She said, "Why, that's so easily taken care of. You make him Secretary of Commerce, and he will be a big man. That position will make him a big man." James and John wanted the big positions. But Jesus said they would have to earn those places of honor, and the one who earned the highest would be the one who served the best. And so, beloved, the Christian life is a continual challenge.

Some time ago I found a story of a man who lived a most unselfish and beautiful life. He lived in a small house on a back street and held no position of importance in his town. He had never done any heroic deeds nor been honored with any medals. If the city had been voting on the most important citizen, they would have entirely overlooked him. That is, they would have overlooked him until the day he died, because then they realized for the first time that this humble man was the first citizen of the township.

When he prayed in church, something happened to people's hearts. Troubled and heartbroken people had beaten a path to his house. It was a long journey for him to walk through the city, because everybody

stopped him just to talk a little or to ask his advice
about something or to tell him of some disappointment.

The day he died the stores did little business, and
little groups of men, with sad faces, could be seen
everywhere talking in low tones. The florist emptied
his greenhouse and banked the funeral parlor with
his choicest flowers. The funeral director from the
next county drove over and offered his services free,
because he said, "I was a drunkard until one day Joe
got hold of me and told me of the saving power of the
Lord." The richest man in town had just bought a new
carriage, and he brought it down to Joe's house as a
gift to his widow.

The tollgate keeper said, "I have been the tollgate
keeper for over thirty years and never before have I
seen twelve hundred carriages come through in one
day." The whole city stopped for the funeral, and
only then did they realize the unselfishness of this man
who had gone down the valley of the shadows to stand
before God's throne for his coronation day.

It was something like this that Jesus had in mind
when he said, "But he that is greatest among you shall
be your servant."

Beloved, that's the thing that Jesus is talking about—
service instead of self-interest. You can be great only
when you overcome the cross pull that's in you, and
instead of selfishness, live a life of helpfulness and
beauty and loveliness, teaching others about Christ
and his power to cleanse from sin and to make life over
again.

6

Needed, but Not Deserved

*For by grace are ye saved through faith;
and that not of yourselves: it is the gift
of God: not of works, lest any man
should boast.*

—Ephesians 2:8-9

Dr. S. M. Lindsay, of Boston, gave me the best working definition of grace that I have ever found. We were in a simultaneous revival at Richmond, Virginia, and Dr. Lindsay was preaching to the preachers. He said to us, "The best definition I have been able to work out for grace is this: *Grace is something that you need but do not deserve.*"

He illustrated it with an experience from his younger days. In substance he said, "I was reared in Scotland, and one year I taught a class of Juniors in the Sunday school. The lesson for a Sunday in April was based on the second chapter of Ephesians, the grace chapter. A number of times I repeated for them this definition for grace, but I was sure it didn't sink in very well.

"The next day I had an engagement in the late afternoon for a formal tea, and so I dressed in striped trousers, cutaway coat, spats, and a high silk hat. It was about a half-mile walk from my house to the village, and one of my boys, Bobby, saw me coming. There was a little wet snow still in the shady places, and my stovepipe hat and the wet snow were a temptation that Bobby couldn't resist. He made a couple of ice snowballs and hid in the boxwood shrub hedge. When I got opposite him he fired away. He missed the hat and hit me in the ear. He surely got results. I saw a cluster of stars, and the hat went sailing into the mud. Bobby was so astonished that he bolted from the shrubs and ran for home with never a backward look.

"When I had recovered somewhat, I was sorely tempted to catch him and thrash him. Then I decided I would just go and tell his father; but then I thought of the Sunday school lesson of yesterday, and I decided to practice grace on him. He needed a fishing pole, for he had borrowed mine the week before, so after the tea I bought him a three-joint rod and took it by his home. I guess Bobby saw me coming, for he was nowhere around the house when I arrived. I gave it to his mother and told her to give it to Bobby for a birthday present and to tell him that I knew his birthday was a month or two off, but I also knew he needed a fishing pole. I asked her particularly to tell him that I *knew he needed* a fishing pole.

"About an hour later, there was a timid knock on my door, and when I opened it, Bobby held the fishing pole out to me. He said, 'I brought your fishing pole back, Mr. Lindsay. I can't take it.'

"And when I asked him, 'Why?' he answered, 'If you had knowed it was me that hit you in the ear with that ice snowball, you wouldn't have give it to me.'

"My answer startled him. I said, 'That's why I gave it to you, Bobby.'

" 'I don't understand, Mr. Lindsay.'

" 'Bobby, what was the Sunday school lesson about yesterday?'

" 'I don't remember.'

"I said, 'It was about grace, and grace is something that you *need* but don't *deserve*.' His eyes brightened, and a slow grin spread over his face as he began to understand.

"I said, 'All right, Bobby—question and answer— What is grace?'

"Like a bolt out of the blue, he answered, 'It's a fishing pole, Mr. Lindsay.'

"I said, 'That's right, Bobby, it's a fishing pole when you *need* a fishing pole and don't *deserve* it.' "

This definition fits beautifully into many places where the word *grace* is used in the New Testament. I was startled to find, as I studied further, how much of the life of Jesus revolved around this great truth.

First, look at the teachings of Jesus. The two most beautiful stories that Jesus ever told have *grace* as their heart and core. In the story of the prodigal son the word *grace* does not appear, but the word *deserve* does. The prodigal son said to himself, "I will go home and tell my father I no longer deserve to be called his

son. Make me as one of the hired servants." Suppose
his father had agreed to that? Then we would have
had no story of the prodigal son. It would not have
been worth telling. I am sure the most wonderful word
that boy ever heard from his father's lips was that
word "son" as the old father told the servants to
bring a robe and some sandals and a ring for his son
that was lost was found. His father gave him not what
he *deserved* but what he *needed*. His great need was not
sandals or a robe, nor was it a ring. His great need
was to hear that dear old father call him "son" and
welcome him home lovingly. The whole beautiful
truth revolves around *grace*.

Look at the story of the good Samaritan. When the
Samaritan went down that road from Jerusalem to
Jericho, he found a Jew that needed something. From
the hands of the Samaritan he didn't deserve anything,
for the Jews treated the Samaritans despicably. When
they passed a Samaritan, they gathered their robes
close about them, got over on the other side of the
road, and spat in the general direction of the Samaritans or sneered and scoffed at them. But this Samaritan
didn't give this Jew what he *deserved*, but what he
needed. He practiced *grace* on him. If, as in the story
of the prodigal son, the Samaritan had not given him
what he needed, there would have been no story. The
whole episode revolves around the word *grace*.

Not only by implication, as in these two illustrations, but by direct statement Jesus filled his teachings
full of grace. In the Sermon on the Mount, in effect he
said, "Love your enemies. Don't give them what they

deserve, but what they *need*. If people despitefully use you and persecute you, don't use them despitefully; don't give them what they deserve, but give them what they need, pray for them. Don't do good just to people who do good to you, but do good to them that do evil to you. Give them what they need. If someone smites you on the right cheek, don't give him what he deserves, but turn the other cheek. If someone compels you to go with him one mile, don't wait for a chance to get even, but go with him two."

Not only in the teachings of Jesus do we find this thought, but we find it throughout the whole Bible.

In 2 Kings we see another illustration of grace. The Syrians were waging war against the Israelites. However, God revealed the plans of the Syrian army to Elisha, who then told the king of Israel. Every time an ambush was laid, Elisha would expose the plan to his king, who would go about to stop it. The king of Syria was so astonished that he called all of his officers together and stated flatly that there must be a traitor. But one of his officers was wiser than the others and told him that Elisha knew the very thoughts that the king expressed in private. Then the king sent a troop to catch Elisha at Dothan. Elisha asked God to blind the enemies, and while they could not see, he told them that they were in the wrong place but that he would lead them to the man they sought. He led them into the heart of the capital and then asked God to open their eyes. The king of Israel was ready to smite them with the sword, but Elisha stopped him. He told him to give them food and treat them kindly and let

them return to their master unharmed. Then read the
last sentence in that story, "So the bands of Syrians
came no more into the land of Israel." Elisha gave
them not what they *deserved* but what they *needed*, and
he ended a war. It's a great principle. It's the secret of
much happiness. It's a pity that it isn't used more
often.

Next, look at the *actions* of Jesus. They also revolve
around this word *grace*. The world didn't deserve for
Jesus to leave his ivory palaces and come to earth and
suffer "the slings and arrows" of mankind, but the
world *needed* Jesus very, very much. One day they
brought a woman taken in sin and flung her down into
the dust in front of Jesus. A crowd gathered around. A
Pharisee asked, "What shall we do with her? Moses in
his law said that a woman like this should be stoned to
death. What do you say?"

I think that Jesus looked at that Pharisee a long time,
and pity and compassion were in his face. Slowly he
stooped and wrote in the dust with his finger and
without looking up quietly said, "Let him that is
without sin first cast a stone." I am sure there wasn't a
word spoken in that crowd for a long time, and I am
sure they silently drifted away.

Then Jesus said to the woman, "Neither do I
condemn thee: go, and sin no more." He gave her
what she *needed*, not what she *deserved*. He practiced
grace on her and in all probability completely changed
her life.

Another day he passed along the Jericho road and
saw a little man looking down on him from a sycamore

tree. With a smile he motioned Zacchaeus to come down and said to this man who didn't deserve to be honored by the most notable person in his world, "I would like to go home with you for lunch." I am sure the cold chills ran up and down the back of Zacchaeus and that his face was flushed and then pale. I am sure he stammered incoherently as he led Jesus to his home. Jesus didn't give this despised publican what he *deserved* but what he *needed*.

But maybe the most beautiful incident of grace in the actions of Jesus was at the end of his earthly life. I saw it at Oberammergau in the Bavarian Alps the last time it was played for the public. The curtain was rolled up slowly. We first saw the feet and lower legs of two strong Roman soldiers, and as the curtain rose a little higher we saw the long, ugly, black bull whips slide back and along the floor and then heard them sing through the air and fall with a sickening thud on someone tied to the whipping post. The whips sang on and the curtain rose higher. Jesus' hands were tied high above his head against the post. His back was bared to the waist; and an ugly X had been cut across his back by the two whips; the blood trickled down over his garments. One of the Roman soldiers dropped his whip and pulled the end of the buckskin thong that tied the hands of Jesus and the Master fell to the ground unconscious. They poured water on him and revived him. They sat him on a wooden bench, and another soldier brought a crown of thorns and gingerly placed it on his head. They put two staves like a plus mark across the crown of thorns. A soldier took each end of the staves and then they counted, *"Eins, zwei, drei,"* and together they pressed down. A moan, heartbreaking, came from the lips of the Master, and the blood ran down his neck and face. They took him away and nailed him to a cross, and then he turned his face to heaven and earnestly prayed, "Father, forgive them, for they know not what they do." Not what they deserved, but what they needed, Jesus gave to them. Sometimes it seems to me his whole life revolved around this one great principle of *grace.*

Last, *what should this mean to us?* Does it mean that Jesus wanted us to make grace a dominating life principle? What a difference that would make! Wars would stop. The heartbreaks in our business would change into smiles. Worries and ulcers would be eliminated. If we practiced *grace* in our homes, the divorce courts would be covered with dust.

Let me close with this illustration. Joseph Parker and Charles Haddon Spurgeon were pastors in the same city. Their personalities were very different. Spurgeon was fiery and quick tempered. Joseph Parker was gentle and sweet spirited. Spurgeon's church ran an orphanage for boys, and one day Joseph Parker said to a group of men, "We ought to help Spurgeon with his orphanage, for there are times when the boys don't have proper clothes, and I am sure they could use some food."

One of the men in that group relayed a half-truth to Spurgeon. He told him that Joseph Parker had said the boys of the orphanage didn't have enough to eat and not enough clothes to wear. On the next Sunday,

Spurgeon berated Joseph Parker from his pulpit and said some very caustic things. A newspaper reporter got hold of it and asked Parker if he intended to answer Spurgeon on the next Sunday. With a smile, the great-souled preacher told the reporter yes, that he would answer Spurgeon. The papers carried the story and the next Sunday Joseph Parker's church was packed. When the time came to receive the morning offering, the minister said, "Mr. Spurgeon is sick today and not in his pulpit. This is the day he takes the offering for the orphanage, and I want to suggest to you that we take the offering for him here in our church, for he is doing a great work, and I am sure we would like to have a part in it."

The plates had to be emptied three times before that offering was completed. The deacons put it in a big bag and took it over to Spurgeon's home and told him what Joseph Parker had said. On the next Wednesday, Spurgeon came to Joseph Parker's study, put his arms around the great-hearted preacher and said to him, "You have more of the spirit of Jesus Christ than any man I know." He had practiced *grace* on Spurgeon and had given him what he *needed*, not what he deserved.

7

Your Life Is What You Make It

*I am come that they might have life, and
that they might have it more abundantly.*

—John 10:10

A successful businessman told the story from
which I have borrowed the title of this message. He
related it something like this:

"I had an appointment at 7:00 P.M. with one of the
big industrialists of our city. I arrived at his home a
little before seven and was ushered into a beautifully
appointed living room. I sat down gingerly in a big
chair. The room was so immaculately clean and
furnished in such excellent taste that I felt a little out
of place. While I waited for the man to finish his
dinner, I looked down at my clothes and wished I
had shined my shoes and shaved and cleaned up a
little. I could hear laughter from the dining room, and
I sat there thinking, 'I have missed something by
being a bachelor and not having a bunch of children
and a nice home of my own.'

58

"My thoughts were interrupted by a five-year-old boy who came dashing from the dining room. He stopped directly in front of me and without a word, looked me over and then said, 'My daddy told me that you were a millionaire. Is that true?'

"I smiled at him and nodded. 'Yes, I guess that's true.'

" 'He said that you are a self-made man, too. Are you?'

" 'Yes, son, I guess I am a self-made man.'

"Once more he looked me over from my dusty shoes to my unkempt hair and then stared me full in the face and said innocently, 'What did you make yourself like that for?' Without waiting for an answer, he bounded out of the room.

"I felt my face turn crimson, and once more I looked with embarrassment at the baggy knees of my trousers and at a necktie that had spots on it; I knew my collar was not fresh and that I needed a haircut. After I had finished my appointment, I went home and took a good look at myself in the mirror. The examination made me very unhappy and led me to take a good look at my whole life. I thought of what the little boy couldn't see—the inside of me was as unkempt as the outside. I sat there in my room a long time and finally got my Bible and had a session with God."

He closed with this sentence: "I guess a man's life is what he makes it."

There is a sense in which we are all self-made men. We choose, sometimes deliberately, sometimes too carelessly, what goes into our lives. We choose these things just as surely as we choose the furniture that goes into our homes. The things that we fondle and caress with our minds become a part of us. The words from Proverbs concerning a man are so true: "As he thinketh in his heart so is he." Our lives are colored and determined by what in college are called "electives." Jesus said of all men, "I came that they might have life and that they might have it more abundantly." He set before us many beautiful precepts and tenets. He made them as attractive as possible, hoping that we would choose these gracious components and enjoy abundant life, for since the choice is ours, the responsibility is ours, also. Our lives are what we make them. Look at three of these choices.

First, we choose what Jesus called our *way of life.* Let me illustrate this way:

Some time ago a woman was invited to speak before a large woman's club and tell them the secret of her happy life. She received a glowing introduction in which the presiding officer asserted that many envied her radiant personality and abundant life. She rose and began to speak.

"I am afraid I am going to startle you when I tell you that *a tramp changed my life.*" Immediately you could have heard that proverbial pin drop. She continued, "I was washing the breakfast dishes one morning when there came a knock at the back door. I opened it and saw a tramp standing there. Very politely and very deliberately he took off his hat and bowed.

" 'Madam,' he said, 'I am ashamed to beg. I have

tried to find work but have failed. I will gladly work for my breakfast, for I am very hungry. Is there something that you have that I can do?'

"I stood there and looked down at him with my arms akimbo and told him in pretty severe tones that I had no patience with tramps and that I never gave them anything. I added, 'You can tell your fellow tramps to stay away from my back door. I work for my living, and you can work for yours. I will not feed you.' When he stood there without moving, still holding his hat in his hands, I scoldingly demanded, 'Go on. Go away. If you don't go, I will call my husband.'

"He slowly raised his head and looked at me and answered, 'Your husband's not at home.'

"It startled me, and I asked, 'How do you know he isn't at home?'

"In a very flat voice he replied, 'If he is home, it's because he's sick. He wouldn't stay home with you unless he was sick.' Then he turned around and very slowly walked away.

"I shut the door and leaned against it. I couldn't finish washing those dishes. After a while I went in and sat down and started thinking about how little my husband did stay at home. I wondered if the tramp was right and if God sent him to bring me to my senses. My thoughts went back over the morning. I had scolded my husband. I had not been kind to him the evening before. A thousand little ugly things raised their heads. I took a good look at myself, and I didn't like what I saw. That day I asked God to help me change my life and fill it full of good things, and today, like Paul, 'I count not myself to have apprehended: but . . . I press on.' "

We choose our way of life. Maybe it would be more often true to say, "We drift into our way of life." Jesus called himself "the way," and I think his voice was very quiet and engaging when he said to those fishermen on the shores of Galilee, "Follow me." His voice comes down through the ages, "Follow me, and I will show you a better way of life." God never drives us into a better way. With all of his power, he uses no force to make us choose the high road. Our lives are what *we* make them.

After we choose our goals in life, then we bend our backs to reach them. If our goals are high and worthy they make life worth while, and we travel the high roads, and we live on the highest levels. *Our lives are all wrapped up in our goals.*

An old, old artist, Dr. Watts, had a three-panel picture to illustrate this. In the first panel there was a young man sitting at his study table at college. He had a book open in front of him, but he wasn't studying. He had turned his student lamp low. He had pushed back his eye shade and with elbows on the table and chin in his hands he was looking not at the book but at a faraway dreamland. High up on the wall in front of him the artist had painted a shadow picture representing his dream. In the picture a man in ranchman's dress sat on horseback on a knoll overlooking a great range covered with cattle. The boy at the desk saw himself as the owner. This was his goal, and a little bit of a smile played over his face as he enjoyed in anticipation the day when he should achieve his goal.

In the second panel the setting was the same, except that the shadow picture on the wall was a busy office. Desks were everywhere, and men were coming and going. At the end of the big room the door to a private office stood open and at the desk within sat the president. The features of the executive and the features of the boy at the table were the same. This was his goal, and a smile of anticipation played across his face.

The last panel I loved the best. A girl sat at her study table. There was something pure and lovely about her face. With a radiant smile she looked at the shadow picture on the wall. In her imagination she saw a campfire in the jungles of Africa. Around the fire sat a group with their black faces turned up to her. They were leaning forward in rapture listening to every word. A missionary with the same lovely features of the student stood with an open Bible in her hand and a winning smile on her face. One hand was lifted as if she were pointing toward heaven and God. This was her goal. Maybe we don't realize enough how our lives are wrapped around our dreams and what a tremendous part they play in making life worth while or making it a shoddy existence. The words of Paul come back to us, "If there is any excellence, think about these things" (RSV).

We choose our *destiny*, also.

Dr. Truett had an experience that he loved to tell: "I was preaching to the lumberjacks in a little church at the foot of the mountains. Those big, husky fellows, dressed in their corduroy pants and checked shirts, trooped down the mountain every evening and became one of the most attentive and responsive audiences I ever had. Many of them accepted Christ as Lord and Redeemer and, unabashed, walked down the aisles to make their professions of faith. Along toward the end of the meeting there was a night when only one young man came forward. He was tall and handsome, about nineteen years of age. We talked a little while after the service. His face was strong and good and honest. The next morning about ten o'clock I saw one of those big lumberjacks coming down the mountain at a reckless speed. When he pulled up in front of my room, I saw he was soaked with perspiration and panting for breath.

" 'Dr. Truett, will you please climb up to first camp with me? The boy that came forward last night was crushed between two logs, and he can't live.'

"In a few minutes I sat down on the ground by the side of him. The doctor had gotten there first and had given him a shot of morphine to ease the pain, but he was still conscious. When he recognized me, his face broke into a smile. He spoke only one sentence before he crossed the Great Divide: 'Dr. Truett, I am so glad I settled it last night.' Then with a trace of a smile still on his face, his whole body shuddered and relaxed, for like Paul, 'the time of his departure was at hand.' "

⌐ Yes, God gives us the freedom to choose our destiny. No one can make our peace with God for us, and no one who has not accepted the salvation that Jesus offers knows the value and the joy of that peace.

In recent years we have learned the value of peace between nations. We have learned the terror of war. We have realized afresh that when there is not peace on earth and good will among men, our cherished plans get upset, and our lives are full of heartaches. The lights have burned all night in many homes because war raged and the bombs dropped in some distant land and a boy's room was empty and his life was in danger. Peace among nations has become one of the most prized and valued commodities of the world. But have we learned the value of peace in our individual lives? There can never be peace until we know our names are written in God's book of life. No one can write our names there for us. No one can bring about a reconciliation between God and us. Our peace with God will be made only when we make it. Our peace and our lives are all wrapped up in each other. It is hard to understand how people will put off this most important matter.

One day after the morning service I went alone to a restaurant for dinner. When the hostess had seated me at a table, a waitress came to bring a menu. As I looked up at her, I smiled and said, "I am glad she placed me at your table, for I have seen you in church."

She answered, "Yes, I go to your church when I go anywhere."

Of course, my next question was, "To what church do you belong?"

Her answer startled me, "I don't belong to any church. Doctor, I am not a Christian, and if I died today I wouldn't go to heaven."

I am afraid my mouth dropped open in astonishment, and quickly I said, "Certainly you don't want to put off so important a matter as this. When can I see you to talk to you about it? This afternoon?"

When she said, "I am on duty until late tonight," I asked, "What about tomorrow?"

She answered, "I start on my vacation tomorrow morning early."

I said, "Your vacation won't be nearly as happy as it could be if your name was written in God's book of life."

I saw her eyes get misty with tears, and she answered in a low voice, "You aren't happy anywhere when you are not saved." Then to hide her tears she left the table quickly and didn't come back for a long time. When she did return, she said, "As soon as I get back from my vacation, I want you to tell me how to be saved."

Why, oh, why, will people live in misery when Jesus stands with outstretched arms pleading, "Come unto me, all ye that labour and are heavy laden, and I will give you rest." "Peace I leave with you; my peace I give unto you: not as the world giveth, give I unto you. Let not your heart be troubled, neither let it be afraid." You can have this peace and rest—salvation for your very own. Your life can have this great anchor and this sweet assurance. Your life is what you make it.

8

Sons of God

---

*But as many as received him, to them
gave he power to become the sons of
God.*

—John 1:12

*For as many as are led by the Spirit of
God, they are the sons of God.*

—Romans 8:14

*And it shall come to pass, that in the
place where it was said unto them, Ye
are not my people, there it shall be said
unto them, Ye are the sons of the living
God.*

—Hosea 1:10

The wide sweep and the deep and beautiful
meaning of these three verses were opened to me by an
experience that Dr. Norman Vincent Peale told recently. In substance he said, "There came into my
counsel room a man who was very nervous. He sat
down and fidgeted, got up and walked across the room
a couple of times, sat down and began to talk rapidly.

" 'Dr. Peale, I am a Christian layman, a business
executive in this city. I live in the suburbs and com-
mute in and out each day. It takes about forty-five
minutes for me to go and come. I've made it a rule for

a good many years, as I come in each morning, to think about my day's work, look at the problems that I may face, and try to find some solution to them. Then in the afternoon as I go back home, I spend the forty-five minutes going over what happened through the day, trying to see what mistakes I've made and how I might have done differently. I've gotten to worrying a great deal about my business, for these are worrying times.

" 'I became so nervous I couldn't sleep; so I went to my physician. He spent about an hour with me and finally said, "You are about the best target I have ever seen for three things: stomach ulcers, high blood pressure, and a heart attack. You are wide open for any of them, or all of them."

" 'I asked him what I should do about it. He answered, "I can't pour medicine into your mind. I would suggest that you go talk to your minister."

" 'So, Dr. Peale, I came to talk to you. Can you give me a prescription?' "

Dr. Peale said, "I let him talk a long time and then said to him, 'Yes, I can give you a prescription, and if you will carry it out, I know it will help you immensely —probably make you well.'

"He eagerly leaned over my desk and said, 'Dr. Peale, what is it?'

"I answered, 'I want you to start with this. I want you to commit to memory three verses of Scripture, and I want you to say them over every morning when you get on that train. During that forty-five minutes think about them or the channels into which they send your thoughts. Say them over when you get on that train in the afternoon. Meditate upon them; get your Bible, and read them, and read the surrounding verses, and don't think about your business at all while you are on that train.

" 'These are the three verses: "As many as *received* him, to them gave he power to become the sons of God." That's the first one. Here is the second: "For as many as are *led by* the Spirit of God, they are the sons of God." And the last one is, "In the place where it was said unto them, Ye are not my people, there it shall be said unto them, Ye are the sons of the living God." ' "

Now, I don't know what else Dr. Peale said to him or what he said to Dr. Peale or what the outcome was, for suddenly I saw a definite progression and a marvelous promise in these passages. I had never noticed how beautifully those verses complement each other in presenting one of the greatest themes in all the Bible or how beautifully they surround it and say it all and leave nothing unsaid.

I would have said to Dr. Peale's Christian businessman something like this, "You will find out if you commit these three verses to memory and say them over often enough there will come into your mind a grand assurance of security, a security that is yours because you belong to God, and God belongs to you, because you're God's son, and God is your Father. And you will come to realize that whatever happens to you, you have a Friend that you can trust to the uttermost, a Friend that never fails, who can do anything, for he created this world, and we are his people. You will find yourself loving the ninety-first Psalm: 'He that dwelleth in the secret place of the most High shall abide under the shadow of the Almighty. . . . Thou shalt not be afraid for the terror by night; nor for the arrow that flieth by day. . . . A thousand shall fall at thy side, and ten thousand at thy right hand; but it shall not come nigh thee. . . . Only with thine eyes shalt thou behold and see the reward of the wicked.' You will not experience it—only see it with your eyes." I think that is what I would have said to him.

So, beloved, if those three verses were good for a man who was getting close to a nervous breakdown, high blood pressure, heart attack, or ulcers of the stomach, they might be good for every Christian to meditate upon and commit to memory. I think we should keep them in the order in which they were stated, for step by step they build to a beautiful climax. Let us notice the progression.

"As many as received him, to them gave he power to become sons of God." The big word in that sentence is *received*. All of God's part in the plan of salvation has been completed. It's finished; just as Jesus said on the cross, "It is finished," the plan of salvation is finished. Our part is to *receive* it. As someone has said, "The saddest words in all the Bible are in the first chapter of John: 'He came unto his own, and his own received him not.' " And it could be said of so many people in this world of ours today, that Jesus came to them in this lovely land, and they received him not. Receptivity is a grace that is hard to find.

Why is it that the world has not received Jesus? I
believe I could tell you two good reasons. One of them
is because inside of every one of us—maybe a double
first cousin to our consciences—there is a distaste and
a dread of inconsistency. We don't like to be inconsistent. We don't like to be one thing before all of our
friends and another thing somewhere else. We don't
like secret sins in ourselves or in others. So, when
Jesus comes and knocks at the door of our hearts, as
Holman Hunt's beautiful painting depicts, and when
he turns his ear to listen to see if there are footsteps on
the inside, we don't open the door. We don't want him
because there is something inside our houses that we
don't want him to see. There is something inside of us
that would be incompatible with the lovely and pure
Christ, and so we don't receive him; and, therefore, we
don't become the sons of God.

You know, there are some places in your city where
a *real* Christian is not welcome. I'm not talking about
over-pious people, now; I'm not talking about snob-
bish people; I'm talking about genuine, down to earth
Christians. There are some places in your community
where they are not welcome; there are circles where
they are not wanted. That's a sad thing. They are not
wanted, because the people are doing things that Jesus
Christ would not like. So he says to them that will *receive* him he will give the power to become the sons of
God. In Zechariah 3:1 you'll find a sentence that reads
that Satan stood at his right hand to resist him. Every
time you start toward that door to receive Christ into
the house in which you live, Satan leans against it. He

is not going to let you open that door to receive Jesus Christ if he can help it, and there are a thousand ways he can help it.

This last week I found a story about which the editor's note said, "This story below has been printed over two million times in the last twenty years." I had never seen it before; maybe you have. It read something like this:

The devil decided to have an auction. He decided to go out of business and sell all his tools. The auction day came, and a great crowd of people gathered. He placed all of his tools out on a red plush mat. The tools were envy, jealousy, greed, avarice, vengeance, resentment, hatred—all of them.

Off to one side, he had a silver wedge. Someone asked him what it was, and he said, "That's a silver wedge. See how bright and shiny it is. I use it all of the time. It's the best tool I have. I put it over there because it's the most valuable. It is worth more than all the other tools put together."

They asked, "Well, how do you use it?"

Satan answered, "That is the wedge of discouragement. You can take the finest Christian, one who has received Jesus Christ into his life and who is trying to serve him, and drive the wedge of discouragement into his Christian work and wreck his usefulness. A Sunday school teacher doesn't see the results he wants. The Sunday school superintendent, Training Union director, and Woman's Missionary Union president, dead in earnest about their work, can often become discouraged. I can drive that wedge in and pry open a door, and all the rest of my cohorts can go in. I can break that life down with discouragement."

After a moment someone asked, "Satan, are there any people in the world that you cannot use that wedge on?"

He answered, "Just one group of people."

And everybody pressed forward to ask, "Who are they?"

"They are the thankful people—the people who have gratitude in their hearts. They are the humble people. They are the people who thank their Heavenly Father for all the blessings of their lives. They are the people who have thrown wide open the doors of their hearts and let Jesus come in." People who know that God is their Father and that they are his children are not easy targets for Satan's silver wedge of discouragement.

But now let us look at our second verse. "As many as are led by the Spirit of God, they are the sons of God." There is another verse very similar to this that beautifully emphasizes the thought. "Now if any man have not the Spirit of Christ, he is none of his." Paul is here contrasting the life that is *led* by the Spirit of God and the life that is *driven* by the law of God. I have never seen a truly beautiful Christian who did not have the Spirit of Christ. This is what Jesus was talking about when he put the emphasis on the "inside of the cup." He did not want people to be praying or fasting because the law said to pray and fast. But he wanted them to pray and fast as a result of a hunger for righteousness and fellowship with God. The publican in the story of Jesus went down justified, rather than the Pharisee, because the Pharisee's prayer received its impulse from the outside, and the publican's prayer boiled up out of a hunger from inside. Anyone that is led by the Spirit of Christ must forever be doing gentle and lovely things.

I found a beautiful illustration of this in *The Reader's Digest*. It went like this: "My friend had put up a sign, 'Puppies for Sale,' and we went out to inspect the litter. Neither of us had seen the boy come up, but suddenly a small voice said, 'Please, mister, I'd like to buy a puppy if they don't cost too much.'

" 'Well, son, they're ten dollars.'

"The child's face fell. 'I only got $1.63. Could I look at them anyway?'

" 'Sure; maybe we can work something out.' He whistled, and Lady trotted out with five little balls of fur rolling along behind her.

"The little boy caught his breath and then said anxiously, 'I heard there was one with a bad leg.'

" 'Yes,' said my friend. 'I'm afraid she's hopelessly crippled.'

" 'That's the one! Could I pay for her a little at a time?'

" 'But wouldn't you rather have one that could play with you?' I asked. 'This one will never be able to walk very well.'

"Hiking up one trousers leg, the little boy showed a brace. 'I don't walk so good either,' he said matter-of-factly, 'and I reckon she'll need some understanding 'til she gets used to it. I did.'

"A happy little boy got his dog; money wasn't mentioned."

Beloved, it isn't enough to receive Jesus Christ into our lives and then just sit down and say, "I have accepted Christ; I have opened the door; I have received him. He has forgiven me for my sins." That isn't enough. We must be *led by his Spirit.* Simon Peter followed Jesus "afar off," and we can follow him so far away that no one will ever know that we are sons or daughters of God. This is the complement to "receiving him." To them he gives the power—the privilege—to be led by the Spirit and become the sons of God. "As many as are led by the Spirit of God, *they are the sons of God.*"

Now, I take the last one, and this is the glorious climax. "In the place where it was said unto them, Ye are not my people, there it shall be said unto them, Ye are the sons of the living God." What happened between these two clauses? Something wonderful happened. One day God said to these people, "Ye are not my people; I turn my back on you; I'll have nothing to do with you." But in the very same place, it was said of them *later* (for the prophecy had become history) "Ye *are* the sons of the living God." What happened in between? Two things happened. They received God, and they were led by his Spirit. Of course, receiving God meant just what it means today. They repented of their sins, and they were forgiven, and then they accepted God's way of life and let him lead them in the path of righteousness. It meant a complete change in their way of living. The words of Jesus in the story of

Nicodemus come back to us, "Ye must be born again."

Some years ago I read an incident that says this so much better than I can. A grand old man of England died. Just before his death, the editor of a New York newspaper got on a plane and went to see him. They were old friends. The editor pulled his chair up beside the bed where the old man was propped up in his pillows. For a minute or two they just sat looking at each other and smiling as they clasped hands, and then they broke out laughing. They had had a lot of good times together.

After they had reminisced a little while, the editor said, "Look, one thing I never did ask you, and I want to know, for it will make good copy for my newspaper when you cross over the Great Divide. Tell me this: what changed your life? You were pretty wild and reckless when you were young. I know, for I was with you. Something changed us both. What changed *you?* Was it that experience with the *Caspar* sinking out there in the ocean when you were standing by, their only hope?"

"Well," the old sea dog answered, "that's where it happened. It was like this. It seemed to be impossible to get anybody off of the *Caspar* before it broke in two. But we got them all off. A half-dozen times we almost went down ourselves, but we got them off. The captain was the last one. When he crawled up that deck ladder and came over the rail of my boat, I was holding his little four-year-old girl.

"His wife ran to him and put both arms around his neck, and with the tears streaming down her face, she said, 'I told you so. I told you that God talked to me just like he talked to Paul, and he told me that nobody was going to be drowned and that we all were going to get off.' Then she turned to me and said, 'Captain, will you just keep on holding my daughter while I get down here on my knees and thank God for saving us?' I told her it was perfectly all right for her to get down and pray, for everybody on my ship had been praying. Just then the *Caspar* broke in two, and we stood silently and watched it sink. Then she got down on her knees and prayed.

"When she held out her arms to her little daughter a moment later, that little daughter just snuggled up closer to me. I had a three or four days' growth of beard, and I don't know how she stood it, but she put her cheek up against mine and said, 'Mother, is this God?'

"Her mother smiled and said, 'Why, no, honey. What made you think he was God?'

" 'Well, you kept saying that God would save us, and this man saved us.'

"After a moment, her mother, still smiling, said, 'No, he is not God. He is just one of God's men that God used today.' "

The old sea captain turned to his boyhood friend with a radiant light in his eyes. "You know, I just decided I would be one of God's men always. He could use me any day; he could use me every day if he wanted me."

How beautifully this illustrates that verse. There was a time when, doubtless, God had said both to the editor and to the old sea captain, "Ye are not my people," but on this day, as they sat talking together, surely God was smiling down on them, and you can almost hear his words, "Ye are the sons of the living God."

9

The Half Way House

Ephraim is a cake not turned.
—*Hosea 7:8*

I recently read a story told by the keeper of the Half Way House near Oberammergau in the Bavarian Alps. It was not a very pretty story, for, using his own words, "My Half Way House is not a happy place, and my job is not a happy job."

He continued about like this: "A great crowd of people will enthusiastically start to climb the mountain. It is a mountain which is made to order for amateurs and tenderfeet. Most of their enthusiasm has vanished by the time they reach my Half Way House. There is a broad expanse of windows on one side that look out across the world below, and the climbers all rush to it with expressions of delight and rave about the beauty of the view. But when they look the other way, up toward the top of the mountain, all of their zeal and zest vanish. They look at the big fireplace with its roaring fire and comfortable chairs and at the refreshment counter with hot coffee and sandwiches and decide they have climbed far enough. About half of them never go any farther. They tell the guide that

they are tired, that their feet are wet, and that the
snow is too deep. So the guide goes on with a part of
his crowd, and the others stay at the Half Way House.

"They are a restless group, but they try to be gay.
They play a little; they sing a little. They are half
repentant; they are half remorseful. Every once in a
while, as if drawn by a magnet, they will go to the big
window and watch the crowd climbing to the top. By
and by everything will grow very quiet, and then one
of them will exclaim, 'They are at the top.' Then
gloom settles over the whole group. When the climbers
return, radiant, laughing, and rosy-cheeked, those who
stayed at the Half Way House are miserable."

When I read this story, my mind immediately
turned to a verse in the seventh chapter of the prophecy of Hosea: "Ephraim is a cake not turned." Hosea
was likening the tribe of Ephraim to a cake of bread
that was placed on the hot coals and was never turned
over. It was edible, but it was not delicious. From the
record, it seems that God had a hard time with
Ephraim. They turned to him and came part of the
way and then stopped and were joined to their idols;
then he forgave them, and they started again, but it
never could be said of them, as it was said of Amaziah,
that "they wholly followed the Lord." They stopped
at the Half Way House.

It seems to me that this is an accurate though dis-
mal picture of American life today. It won't make us
happy, but it might do us good to think of these three
things:

First, there are many *Christian* people who live at

the Half Way House. They are people whose names are written in God's book of life. They are people who have accepted Jesus Christ as their Lord and Saviour and have been saved, *are* saved, *will be* saved. They are people who have made a profession of faith, have been baptized, who go to church, and yet live in the Half Way House. They have never surrendered completely, entirely, to God. Their lives have some reservations in them; there is compromise in their ethics, in their behaviour, in their way of life, in the places to which they go, the things they do, and in the things they leave undone. Some have great talents, fine personalities, and superb abilities, but they refuse to dedicate these to God's use. There are many people with fine minds, keen intellects, and a splendid knowledge of God's Word, but they won't teach a Sunday school class, lead in Training Union, or take their places in the missionary program of the church.

There are others who have many possessions but are like the rich young ruler and turn away sorrowfully when God wants their silver and their gold. There are many who seem to think they have a better plan than God's plan for financing the kingdom's objectives. They have never given God a chance to show what he meant in the third chapter of Malachi, where he said, "Bring ye all the tithes into the storehouse, that there may be meat in mine house, and prove me now herewith, saith the Lord of hosts, if I will not open you the windows of heaven, and pour you out a blessing, that there shall not be room enough to receive it." These people have missed the joy of their salvation. They could have gone on to the top. They could have been Christians of the first magnitude. They could have heard the music and felt the thrill of God's voice saying, "This is my beloved Son, in whom I am well pleased."

There are others who live in the Half Way House because they have never felt any responsibility for taking the sweetest story ever told to the unsaved. They have never realized that God needs individual, personal instruments to do his work and that every one of us has a place in the great task of evangelism and missions.

Let me illustrate: Mark Guy Pierce said, "The greatest and strangest revival I ever had a part in happened this way. I had preached two weeks in one place without one single profession of faith. Then the last night one little girl came forward on the invitation hymn. I was so glad to see her that I talked to her a little longer than I usually do. I told her that God is able to forgive sins and wipe out the past, and then he is able to keep us from doing anything wrong any more. We can trust him and not be afraid for the rest of our lives. We closed the service, at least my part of it. But the real revival began the next Sunday, for on the next day a man came to this little girl's house to see her father, who wasn't at home.

"When she opened the door, he smiled and said to her, 'You are all dressed up this morning. Are you going somewhere?'

"She answered, 'No, sir. I dressed up because I'm happy. You see, last night I became a Christian, and the preacher told me that God had the power to wipe out all of my sins, and that he could keep me from ever doing wrong again. He told me I had nothing to be afraid of because God would watch over me.' Then she looked up into his face and said, 'Are you a Christian?'

"When he answered, 'No,' she asked him why.

"He fidgeted for a minute and then pointed across the street to the blacksmith shop and said, 'Honey, I don't doubt for a minute that God has the power to keep *you* and take care of *you*, but before I become a Christian I am going to have to be convinced that God could save and change a man like Old Dan, the blacksmith. He is the meanest cuss that ever lived. The day when Old Dan goes to church and is saved and God promises to take care of him and keep him from doing anything that's wrong, that day I'll go to church.' "

Mark Guy Pierce said, "The little girl sat on the front steps and listened to the ring of Old Dan's hammer a long time, and then she marched herself over there. The gruff old giant, stripped to the waist, swinging his hammer, heard a voice behind him. 'Dan!' He stopped, turned around, and there she stood, all prim and beautiful.

"He said, 'What do you want?'

"She said, 'Dan, could I talk to you a minute?' When he had finished what he was doing, he sat down by her, and she told him why she had come. She told him what had happened a few minutes before, and then with her little white hand on his big, brawny black one, she said, 'Dan, please come to church next

Sunday so that people will believe that Jesus was able to save me and save anybody. Please come to church next Sunday.'

"Old Dan promised he would come to church next Sunday. And when that little town heard that Old Dan, the blacksmith, was at church, it was news. The next Sunday came, and half a hundred people went to church just to see if Old Dan was coming again, and sure enough, he was there."

Mark Guy Pierce choked, and then with a voice full of emotion he added, "God did save Old Dan, and such a revival broke out in that town as had never been seen before—all because one little girl didn't stop at the Half Way House but went on to do what God wants every one of us to do—take the story of God's power to someone else and experience the joy of salvation."

Second, there are too many nominally Christian homes that are only Half Way Houses. The father and the mother, to be sure, have been loyal and faithful to the marriage vows. The father is a good provider; the home is nicely furnished; there is food and clothing for every one. Also, the mother keeps the house beautifully; everything is well organized, and all of the physical wants are supplied. Still it is like a Half Way House because kindness is lacking, and the Spirit of Jesus Christ and the gospel are not adorned in that house. There is no family altar; prayers are not heard; and Jesus would not feel at home as he did in the home of Martha and Mary and Lazarus. The things that are lacking are sweetness and happiness and love. The great intangible values are missing. They have every-

thing in the house to make it a little bit of heaven—
everything except the Spirit of Jesus. God so wisely
had Solomon write down, "Words fitly spoken are like
apples of gold in pictures of silver."

The most startling illustration I ever found of the
value and the need of kindness was an experiment
carried out at the Kellogg Sanitarium, Battle Creek,
Michigan, by Dr. Caroline Geisel. In substance she
said, "There came to the building where we lived and
worked the cutest little pup I ever saw. We all fell in
love with him. He was so anxious to show us his appreciation of our affection that he wagged his tail with
such enthusiasm that his whole body wagged along
with it. He was the happiest pup I ever saw. Any little
thing that we did for him made him bubble over in
response. We took him into the operating room, gave
him an anesthetic, and made an incision in one of his
hind legs. The marrow in the bone was a beautiful
pink, filled with red corpuscles. We carefully bound up
the wound, and it healed almost overnight.

"Then we passed the word around that no one was
to smile at the pup or speak in a kind tone of voice for
six weeks. We fed him just as we always had, but nobody petted him or showed any affection. The poor
little pup just wilted. He became the most forlorn
little dog I ever saw. He crept into the dark corners,
and his tail dragged the ground. We took him back to
the operating room and examined the marrow in the
same bone. It was a brownish color, and the red
corpuscles were very scarce. It took the wound a long
time to heal, despite the fact that we showered all of

our pent-up affection on the little puppy. He responded very slowly to our overtures, and it took a long, long time to get him to wag his tail again. When his enthusiasm was finally restored, we took him once more to the operating room and found the marrow in the bone was pink and beautiful again."

Dr. Geisel said, "The whole world needs to learn the lesson that our physical well-being is dependent upon the peace and happiness of our minds." To me there is an even greater lesson in the story. Doesn't it answer the question why Jesus spent so much time talking about love and going the second mile and praying for our enemies? There are too many houses in this world that are not homes. They are like Ephraim, a cake not turned.

Third, there are many people in this world who fully expect to be Christians, but they have stopped at some Half Way House. They don't intend to stay there. They fully intend to become Christians some day, but it's easier not to do it right now. It is much simpler just to stand still and sing the last verse of the invitation hymn without moving out into the aisle. Some of them have the false idea that when they become Christians, they will no longer be able to enjoy life. Too many follow the lines of least resistance and find it much more comfortable to wait till some more convenient season. So often they write themselves a promissory note. They promise God and whisper to that still small voice inside their souls that they will make a profession of faith, join the church, and go to work for God in the near future. There comes to them a little peace of mind, but the days pile up into years while they sit in ease by the comfortable fire in the Half Way House.

I was greatly moved when I heard Dr. Truett tell this experience: "I rode to a funeral with a fine businessman of Dallas. His youngest daughter was in the hearse. He wanted me to ride in his buggy so he could talk to me, and this is about what he said: 'When you first came to Dallas, fifteen years ago, I went every Sunday morning to hear you preach. Every week I was so upset that I could hardly keep from walking down the aisle and taking my place with you. When I left the church, I was so disturbed that I didn't want anything to eat. Sometimes I walked the streets for hours, and usually I promised myself and God that on next Sunday I would join the church. Then the pain would ease a little, and I would go and get a belated dinner. This kept up for a long time, and I can't remember when that urge to be a Christian ceased. I go to hear you preach quite often now, but I never feel like I did then. You certainly are a better preacher than when you first came here; so something must have happened to me. Can you explain it?' "

Dr. Truett said, "It nearly broke my heart for I couldn't bear to tell this man what really had happened." All of us know how easy it is to harden our hearts or let Satan harden them against God. So many people stop too soon in their battle against the wrong; so many others stop too soon in their climb to reach a right and beautiful fellowship with God.

There is a Half Way House in every block in this

great country of ours. There are people in every crowd who have made Half Way Houses of their homes. I wonder if this is not the cause of so much misery in our world? There is a sad note in the voice of God as he says, "Ephraim is a cake not turned." Beloved, I beg of you not to make the Half Way House your home. God has in store for you a place on top of the world that Jesus called "abundant life," if you will make your surrender to him complete and unconditional.

10

Three Ways of Life

> *A man's life consisteth not in the abundance of the things he possesseth.*
> —*Luke 12:15*

I am indebted to Dr. David Gardner, editor emeritus of the *Baptist Standard*, for showing me something that I had never seen before in the story that Jesus told about the good Samaritan.

In this story and in it alone Jesus has portrayed for us the three great ideologies or philosophies that predominate in this world. I have preached many sermons from the story of the good Samaritan, but until then I never realized what a perfect picture it is of the motives and the forces which dominate the actions of man. The three ideas can be expressed in a sentence of five words. We only need to change the position of the words in the sentence. Here they are. *What is thine is mine. What is mine is mine. What is mine is thine.*

The first one, *What is thine is mine*, is portrayed by the attitude and the actions of the thieves and robbers. Evidently they saw this Jew before he left Jerusalem, and they saw the purse of coins that he had. They looked at it and then looked at each other; a knowing nod and an understanding smile passed between them which meant, "What he has we will take, and we will get it before he gets to Jericho." That is the philosophy of life that has led to many of the wars. Nietzsche was its most important advocate; Hitler was its apt scholar; Mussolini was an imitator of the same ideology. Stalin and communism adopted it lock, stock, and barrel. Probably none of them ever heard the words of Jesus, "A man's life consisteth not in the abundance of the things he possesseth." If they heard it, they could not understand it, or else they rejected it in toto.

Charles Wells, syndicate reporter who travels over the world and has a mind keen enough to interpret the things that he sees, spoke to the students assembled at Ridgecrest twenty years ago and prophesied a thing that has come startlingly true. He began his message without speaking a word. A long piece of paper, tacked to the blackboards, reached halfway across the platform. He took crayons and quickly sketched a map of Europe and Asia. Little cross marks indicated the places where oil and coal and iron and many other natural resources were deposited. When he had finished the map, he turned to the two thousand students who sat attentively and said in substance, "The wars of the world are fought for the natural resources and the power which they bring. They are started by people who follow the teaching of Nietzsche which essentially is this: 'Take what you can and hold it as long as you can.' "

After a few minutes of lecturing, he turned back to the board and with a red crayon drew a curved line which marked the southern border of Siberia. He let the end of the line extend to Moscow. Then with a swift stroke of the same red crayon, he drew another line parallel to it. It made a perfect sword. The tip of it was on the shore of the Pacific, the grip was at Moscow. Then he turned back to us and said, "One day there will come a man with strength enough to hold that sword in Moscow and sweep it down across Asia and into Europe. His governing ideology will be [though he did not use these words] *What's thine is mine.*"

The same spirit that possessed the robbers in the story Jesus told—the same spirit that dominates international thieves—is the spirit that governs a great many people in civilized America. Not many professional men or industrialists or business executives would admit to this crude expression of their creed and ethics, but their lives and their actions say exactly this: "What is thine is mine, if I can get it." Nor is this spirit confined to business and international affairs alone, for we find it even in homes and churches. People strive not only for the money that belongs to others, but for the position, the prestige, and the honor. It is indeed a wicked ideology and has nothing of Christianity in it. Socialism looks around at people who have piled up possessions and gained honors and says, "They are no better than we are. Let's get together and bring them down to our level. These executives sit in their luxurious homes and wear their white collars while we do the work and live by the sweat of our brows." Thus capital and labor fight;

and thus nations fight—all because the same grasping philosophy that controlled the thieves on the Jericho road is leavening our world today.

The Levite and the priest present the second ideology. Their actions and their attitude say, *What's mine is mine*—and I'll keep it. As they passed by they looked at the wounded man and thought, "He needs my help; he needs some of my wine and oil for his wounds; he needs some of my time; he needs my beast to carry him down to Jericho. Since he has been robbed, he needs some of my money to pay his hotel expenses, but *what's mine is mine, and I'll keep it.*" You can see them grip the top of their moneybags a little more tightly and hide them in their robes.

Jesus hit hard at this way of life. He told the story of the rich man and Lazarus. The rich man never did anything ugly to Lazarus. He didn't whip him; he didn't even drive him away from his gate; he just shrugged his shoulders and thought, "He needs help, but he won't get any from me, for *what's mine is mine, and I'll keep it.*" Again, when the rich young ruler came and knelt at Jesus' feet and asked, "What shall I do that I may inherit eternal life?" Jesus told him to obey the commandments, and he answered, "All these have I observed from my youth." Then Jesus suggested to him, "Sell whatsoever thou hast and give to the poor . . . and follow me." And the rich young ruler turned away sorrowfully and said, not using these words, but he might as well have used them, "What's mine is mine, and I'll keep it."

The prodigal son said, in substance, the same thing:

"Give me what's mine, and I'll do with it as I like." And though he didn't say it, he was also thinking, "My life is mine, and I'll live it as I please." We all know it isn't as simple as that. We know the Bible is true when it tells us that no man lives to himself. We know that this applies not only to the material side of life, but to life itself. I went to the jail three times recently to see three different boys, all of whom had with their actions said the same thing the prodigal son said, "It's my life; I am twenty-one, and I'll live it as I please." Can't we see the fallacy of that? A boy goes to jail and a mother and a father sit in my study brokenhearted, disgraced in the eyes of their neighbors, and ashamed to come to church—all because a boy says, "What's mine is mine, and I will do with it as I please."

A fellow pastor told me not long ago of an incident that happened to him. He said, "I went down to the five-and-ten cent store with my wife the other day, and while she was finishing her shopping, I leaned against the counter with an arm full of packages. A little boy, dirty and ragged, came in and stood looking longingly at the candy behind the glass showcases. I reached in my pocket and got a quarter, and I handed it to the lady behind the counter and said, 'Give that boy a quarter's worth of candy, and let him pick it out.'

"She smiled and said to the boy, 'All right, son, what do you want?' He went along and picked it out, and when she handed the bag to him, he crammed his mouth full of candy.

"I asked, 'Is it good?'

"He said, 'Uh huh. Uh huh,' his mouth too full to talk.

"I held out my hand and said, 'How about letting me have a piece?'

"The expression on his face changed to one of fear and defiance, and he whirled around and clutched the candy bag and uttered two words: 'Mine! Mine!' He dashed out of the store as fast as he could run."

I wonder if any of us treat God that way? He gives us so many things and then asks that we give some of it back to him in the only way we can give to God, namely, that we help someone else who needs it. I wonder if some of us practice the ideology of the priest and the Levite without realizing our selfishness? You can cover a multitude of sins with one single word— the word *selfishness*. I would to God that we could find this fearful way of life only on the road to Jericho, and not in homes, even Christian homes. I would to God that this philosophy only reared its ugly, vicious head among the nations instead of among people who have named the name of Christ and yet say to God, "What's mine is mine, and I will keep it."

The last idea is the beautiful one. Jesus chose to portray it with a Samaritan. The actions of the Samaritan say distinctly, "What's mine is thine, since you need it. My beast of burden, my oil and wine, my time and care, my compassion and sympathy, and my purse for your expenses at Jericho—all of these are mine, but I give them to you because you need them." Beloved, that's close to the heart of the gospel of Jesus Christ. When God sent Jesus down into this wicked world, his actions said, "This is my beloved Son, and I give him to you because you need him. You are all like sheep gone astray; you have sinned and you have nothing with which to make an atonement. Therefore, I give him to you that you may not have to pay the penalty of your own iniquity. I give him to you that the words of the prophet Isaiah may be fulfilled, 'Though your sins be as scarlet, they shall be as white as snow; though they be red like crimson, they shall be as wool.' I give him to you that you may ask anything in his name and receive it." This is so close to the heart of the gospel. "What's mine is thine" is the Christ-like attitude. This is the Christian way of life.

A businessman of San Antonio, one of the grandest Christians I ever knew, came over to my home late one night about two weeks after Christmas. As I opened the door I asked him, "What brings you out this time of evening?"

Smilingly he answered, "I've got to tell you something that made this Christmas the most wonderful one of my life." He got comfortable before the fire and began. "About four weeks ago my brother gave me a Packard automobile for a Christmas present. One evening a few days before Christmas, I came down out of my office and walked over to my car. There was a little street urchin walking around it touching it with a finger and looking in the windows. When I put the key in the door, he came around on my side. He was ragged and dirty and barefooted.

"He squinted up at me and said, 'Is this your automobile, mister?'

"I smiled at him and said, 'It sure is, son. Isn't it a beauty?'

" 'Mister, what did it cost?'

"When I told him I didn't know, he looked me up and down carefully and then spoke. 'Mister, you don't look like a man that would steal an automobile. Where did you get it?'

"With a bit of pride I told him, 'My brother gave it to me for a Christmas present.'

" 'You mean—' he said, 'you mean your brother gie it to you, and it didn't cost you nothing?'

"I said, 'That's right. My brother gie it to me, and it didn't cost me nothing.'

"He dug his toes down against the sidewalk for a minute and was lost in thought, then he began, 'I wist'—I knew what he was going to wish. He was going to wish he had a brother like that, and I had the answer ready for him. But he didn't say that, and what he did say jarred me all the way down to my heels. 'I wist I could be a brother like that.'

" 'What did you say?' I asked in astonishment.

"He repeated, 'I wist I could be a brother like that.'

"It confused me so that I couldn't find an answer, and I blurted out, 'Don't you want to ride in my automobile?'

"He looked at his clothes and answered, 'It's so pretty and clean, and I'm so dirty I would muss it up.'

" 'You might be dirty on the outside, but you're mighty clean on the inside. You will do my automobile good. Get in.'

"He wanted to know what everything on the panel

board was, and I sat there and explained it to him. We hadn't gone far when he turned and with his eyes aglow said, 'Mister, would you mind driving in front of my house?' I smiled a little as I squeezed the big car down a half-alley and a half-street. I thought I knew what he wanted. I thought he wanted to show his neighbors that he could ride home in a big automobile, but I had him wrong again.

"He pointed ahead and said, 'Stop right where those two steps are. Will you stay here,' he asked, 'till I come back? It will be just a minute.' He ran up the steps, and then in a little while I heard him coming back, but he was not coming fast. He was coming down like he was carrying a load and putting his best foot down first and then the other one even with it. On the steps that came down on the inside I saw his feet first, and then I saw two more feet, withered and dangling. He was carrying his little brother. Infantile paralysis was written all over him. The well boy set his brother down on the bottom step and then sat down by him, sort of squeezed him up against him and pointed to the car.

" 'There she is, Buddy, just like I told you upstairs. His brother gie it to him, and it didn't cost him a cent, and some day I'm gonna gie you one.'

"I slowly climbed out and sat down by them. 'So that's the reason,' I said, 'that you wanted to be a brother like that?'

" 'Yes,' he answered. 'You see, the store windows are full of pretty things, and I try to remember them, but I can't tell him about them very well, and some

day I'm gonna gie him a car so he can see them himself.'

"I said to them both, 'We won't wait until then. I'm
going to put you both in the car and let you see them
today, and I am going to let you pick out anything you
want, and I'll buy it for you.' I put a Christmas tree
up in that house and played Santa Claus for them. It
was the grandest Christmas I ever had." He had
learned what Jesus meant when he said, "It is more
blessed to give than to receive."

The Jericho road runs 'round the world. We all
walk down it. Can you say with Jesus, "What's mine
is thine, *any time you need it?*"

11

Not a Spirit of Fear

*For God hath not given us the spirit of
fear; but of power, and of love, and of
a sound mind.*

—*2 Timothy 1:7*

Kathleen Norris wrote for *The Reader's Digest*
a most interesting article on happiness. In substance
she said, "I was attending a beautiful wedding recently, and on every side I heard people wishing the
bride and groom happiness. Happy, happy, happy
seemed to be the center of every sentence. Behind me
I heard a voice say, 'I am sure they will be happy. She
is so lovely and he is so handsome.' Then another,
'They are bound to be happy; their parents have
given them a nice car and a lovely home.' And someone added, 'He has such a fine position.' In my mind
was ringing, 'Fools, fools, fools. Won't people ever
learn that happiness is not made up of houses and
cars, positions and looks.' Happiness is the result of
intangible things. It's the harvest of thoughts, attitudes, and lovely living. Jesus taught that the kingdom
of heaven is within us and is not made up of material
things."

It is something like this that Paul wrote to Timothy. He loved Timothy. He called him his son—his spiritual son. I am sure he wanted him to be happy as well as useful, so he reminded him that God gave him a basket full of jewels—jewels that were not mined from the earth, but were fashioned in heaven.

"Timothy," he said, "God hath not given us the spirit of fear; but of power, and of love, and of a sound mind." This same thought runs through all the writings of Paul. It seems to me that it was his favorite theme—no fear, but power and love and peace, or a sober mind. Look at these four jewels carefully.

First, "God hath not given us the spirit of fear." Someone recently said that the two greatest enemies to abounding life are Fear of the Past and Fear of the Future. The Fear of the Past centers around guilt. It did not have to be written in the Bible that "your sins will find you out" and that "With what measure ye mete it shall be measured to you again." I repeat, it did not have to be written in the Bible for us to know that this was true. God left a witness of this great truth in our hearts. How often have I heard men say, "I deserve this and worse," or "I had it coming to me." Men without God live in constant fear of the past.

They likewise live in fear of the future. Uneasiness, fretfulness, and worry are the close companions of people who have not anchored their souls in God. One of the glorious things about Jesus and Paul was that they were fearless. Quietly, with beautiful poise, they walked along the dangerous pathway of life with perfect assurance. They were anchored to the great rock-ribbed truth that *this is God's world*. "And we know that all things work together for good to them that love God, to them who are the called according to his purpose."

Second, God has given us the spirit of power. When we think of power as a gift from God, we naturally think in this modern age of atomic power, of the power that God put into that tiny atom and hid in the earth. It's ours. He gave us the earth and told us to have dominion over the atoms, the molecules and the animals, the air, the sea and the land. Or we think of power in terms of turbines, locomotives, or electric plants. But I wonder if there is any power on earth comparable to the power it takes to make a life over. We sometimes call such power being born again, or we call it conversion; but call it anything that we may, it is the power that Paul had in mind. It is the power to take a man that's living wrong and help him to live right. It is the power to take a man who is breaking confidence with all of those who are leaning upon him and change the inside of him, change his attitudes, and change his whole life. We can find a little inkling of how hard that is in the Old Testament where the prophet implies that it is just about as hard for a man to change his ways as it is for a leopard to change his spots. So it takes this gift of God's power; there is no other way. A man *must* be born again. When a man is born again his whole perspective is transformed. The problems that seemed insoluble suddenly have a new light thrown on them, and the experiences that seemed so dark and so dire may be blessings in disguise.

Dale Carnegie in his book, *How to Stop Worrying and Start Living* [1] tells about dropping in one day at the University of Chicago and asking the Chancellor, Robert Maynard Hutchins, how he kept from worrying. The Chancellor replied, "I have always tried to follow a bit of advice given to me by the late Julius Rosenwald, President of Sears, Roebuck and Company, 'When you have a lemon, make a lemonade.' "

Then Carnegie gave two splendid illustrations. He said, "Here is an interesting and stimulating story of a woman I know who did just that. Her name is Thelma Thompson, and she lives at 100 Morningside Drive, New York City. 'During the war,' she said, as she told me of her experience, 'during the war, my husband was stationed at an Army training camp near the Mojave Desert, in California. I went to live there in order to be near him. I hated the place. I loathed it. I had never before been so miserable. My husband was ordered out on maneuvers in the Mojave Desert, and I was left in a tiny shack alone. The heat was unbearable—125 degrees in the shade of a cactus. Not a soul to talk to but Mexicans and Indians, and they couldn't speak English. The wind blew incessantly, and all the food I ate, and the very air I breathed, were filled with sand, sand, sand!

" 'I was so utterly wretched, so sorry for myself, that I wrote to my parents. I told them I was giving up and coming home. I said I couldn't stand it one minute longer. I would rather be in jail! My father

[1] Dale Carnegie, *How to Stop Worrying and Start Living* (New York: Pocket Books, Inc., 1948) pp. 145–146.

answered my letter with just two lines—two lines that
will always sing in my memory—two lines that completely altered my life:

> *Two men looked out from prison bars,*
> *One saw the mud, the other saw the stars.*

" 'I read those two lines over and over. I was
ashamed of myself. I made up my mind I would find
out what was good in my present situation; I would
look for the stars.

" 'I made friends with the natives, and their reaction
amazed me. When I showed interest in their weaving
and pottery, they gave me presents of their favorite
pieces which they had refused to sell to tourists. I
studied the fascinating forms of the cactus and the
yuccas and the Joshua trees. I learned about prairie
dogs, watched for the desert sunsets, and hunted for
seashells that had been left there millions of years ago
when the sands of the desert had been an ocean floor.

" 'What brought about this astonishing change in
me? The Mojave Desert hadn't changed. The Indians
hadn't changed. But I had. I had changed my attitude
of mind. And by doing so, I transformed a wretched
experience into the most exciting adventure of my life.
I was stimulated and excited by this new world that
I had discovered. I was so excited I wrote a book
about it—a novel that was published under the title
Bright Ramparts. . . . I had looked out of my self-
created prison and found the stars.' Life handed her
a lemon so she made a lemonade.' "

The second illustration read: [2] "I once visited a

[2] *Ibid.*, p. 147.

happy farmer down in Florida who turned even a
poison lemon into a lemonade. When he first got this
farm, he was discouraged. The land was so wretched
he could neither grow fruit nor raise pigs. Nothing
thrived but scrub oaks and rattlesnakes. Then he got
his idea. He would turn his liability into an asset: he
would make the most out of those rattlesnakes. To
everyone's amazement, he started canning rattlesnake
meat. When I stopped to visit him a few years ago, I
found that tourists were pouring in to see his rattlesnake farm at the rate of twenty thousand a year. His
business was thriving. I saw poison from the fangs of
his rattlers being shipped to laboratories to make anti-
venom toxin; I saw rattlesnake skins being sold at
fancy prices to make women's shoes and handbags.
I saw canned rattlesnake meat being shipped to custo-
mers all over the world. I bought a picture postcard
of the place and mailed it at the local post office of the
village, which had been rechristened, 'Rattlesnake,
Florida,' in honor of a man who had turned a poison
lemon into a sweet lemonade."

These two stories beautifully exemplify the meaning
of Paul's words, "We are more than conquerors."
He is saying that God not only breaks the shackles,
but he gives us power to turn our imprisonments into
blessings. He demonstrated it in his own life. Even
while he was chained to a soldier, he turned the Roman Empire upside down. They put him in jail, and
he converted the jailer. God wants to teach us to take
the frustrations and disappointments of life and make
something sweet and beautiful out of them.

NOT A SPIRIT OF FEAR

Third, God has given us a spirit of love. One of the delegates to the United Nations General Assembly, Francis B. Sayre, speaking of Jesus said, "That man—Christ—manifested with convincing force, as nobody else in history has ever been able to do, what God—the great God who made the world—is like. He revealed God, the all-powerful, as a being of supreme love—all gentleness, as understanding as a human father. Prophetic souls before him had coupled God with supreme power, but never with supreme tenderness and love, as Christ did. Profound insight—or audacious folly. This revolutionary conception has upset kingdoms and changed the course of empires. It has generated more irresistible power than any other force in history. Great armies, incomparable arrays of material strength, have not been able to withstand it. Today, twenty centuries after his death, his unforgettable words still ring across the world with resurgent, revitalizing power." Everything in Christ's life revolved around goodness, gentleness and love.

Recently I read in a biography of Abraham Lincoln that when the message came to him at Washington that Lee was about to surrender, the President came down to Richmond. Then the biographer did a strange thing. He left out everything that Lincoln did in Richmond except these two incidents. He said, "The President went immediately to the office of Jeff Davis, which, of course, was being guarded by Federal soldiers. Lincoln asked to be left alone in Jeff Davis' office for a little while. As his aides closed the door, he walked over and sat down at the desk of the president of the Confederacy. Two hours later they became a little uneasy and softly opened the door into the big office. The great, lanky President of the United States was sitting in Davis' chair, his arms folded, his fingers entwined, his forehead resting on his hands and his great frame shaking with sobs. He loved both the North and the South. He was thinking of the 600,000 of the country's finest men who had been sacrificed to the god of war. He was thinking of the ties of love and friendship that had been shattered. He was praying to God to help him bind up the wounds, mend the hurts and bring happiness back to his country. With all of his great, loving heart, he was pleading for wisdom.

The other incident was Lincoln's visit to the home of an old friend, George Pickett. It was the Pickett who led the famous charge at Gettysburg. When a lady answered his knock at the door, he took off his black felt hat and said, "Are you George Pickett's wife?"

"Yes," she answered.

He said, humbly, "I'm Abe Lincoln."

Her eyes flew wide open, "You mean that you are President Lincoln?"

In a low voice he answered, "No, I'm just Abe Lincoln, George's old friend."

She said, "He's not here."

Mr. Lincoln replied, "I know he isn't, but I wanted to meet his wife and see his home and the boy." At the sound of his kind voice, the little two-and-a-half year-old son of George Pickett came from behind his mother's skirts and lifted his arms for Abe Lincoln to take him up.

Mrs. Pickett said, "Little George gave the President a big, dewy kiss and immediately both faces lighted up in a smile."

The President said, "George, tell your daddy, that lovable old rascal, that I forgive him everything and I love him just like I always did and the war is not going to make any difference between us. Tell him that for me."

It's a love like that that Paul often describes—a love for others that can come only from God. Despite the things that happen, despite the upsets, despite the things that we have done that displease him, God so loved us "that he gave his only begotten Son" for us. To further emphasize his purpose Jesus told the story of the prodigal son.

Fourth, he gives us a sober mind. This sobriety isn't set over against a mind intoxicated by liquor necessarily, but it is set over against intoxication. The mind may be intoxicated with greed for money, with ambition, with hatred, with prejudice, or with anger. Last week I saw an individual whose mind was so intoxicated that murder throbbed in his heart. He was not drunk on liquor. He was drunk on hate. Paul contrasts with that a quiet mind, a mind at peace with God, with itself, and with all mankind. This is a smiling mind, a happy mind, not an irritated, turbulent mind, but one that's filled with sweet assurance that all is right with the soul—that there is nothing between the soul and the Saviour.

The president of one of the oldest theological seminaries in America, Dr. Joseph Richard Sizoo, one of the most thoughtful authors of our day said, "There was a day when the load was too hard to bear. I went to my study and shut the door and got the Bible. I laid it down in front of me on the desk and let it drop open. The first verse that my eyes lighted on was this, 'He that sent me is with me: the Father hath not left me alone.' I sat there and looked at it and looked at it and looked at it. I said, 'God, I reckon you sent me in here. I reckon you made it open right there. I'm going to take that as mine today and forever.' " Dr. Sizoo went on to say, "Down through these twenty-odd years I have never felt like I felt that day. Whenever troubles pile up, I've said my favorite verse over and over again. 'He that sent me is with me: the Father hath not left me alone.' "

That's a quiet mind. That's the way to have a quiet mind. Make peace with God. Use the power that he offers to make your life what it ought to be. Accept his power of redemption and his love. Take your place in his ranks. Stay close to him.

12

The Balanced Life

And I saw another mighty angel come down from heaven, clothed with a cloud: and a rainbow was upon his head, and his face was as it were the sun, and his feet as pillars of fire: And he had in his hand a little book open: and he set his right foot upon the sea, and his left foot on the earth.
—Revelation 10:1-2

Dr. Archibald Rutledge in his beautiful little book, *An Angel Standing*, has broken open this passage of Scripture and revealed some beautiful gems. He states that to him this presents the finest picture o: the beauty of the balanced life that is to be found anywhere in the Bible. The scene is dramatic. An angel comes down from the heavens and without a word spoken takes his position with his left foot on the earth and his right foot on the sea, and in his hands he holds a little book. It is as if God says, "This is the posture that is needed; this is the way to stand if we would attain to the finest balance in life and if we would find what Jesus called abundant life.

Does not the earth represent the solid importance of material things of life?

Does not the sea represent the depth and the eternity of the spiritual things? Does it not stand for the invisible realities, the imponderable value of truth, righteousness, and faith in God?

Does not the little book represent the heart of the teachings of Jesus? Did God mean to give us here in symbol and picture the key to living the most joyous and fullest and happiest life?

All three of the symbols in this picture are important for the abundant life. Jesus was continually asking, "Wouldst thou be whole?" The New Testament often repeats the phrase, "filled full." Here's the picture of a man keeping the proper balance between the material world and the spiritual world. He is standing erect, one foot resting on the spiritual, one on the material, and in his hands a little book, open to the heart of the teachings of Jesus. Omit any part of the relationship, and a man will never measure up to the pattern on the Mount. Look closely at the three parts of this picture.

First, notice the little book. "And I went unto the angel, and said unto him, Give me the little book. And he said unto me, Take it, and eat it up; and it shall make thy belly bitter, but it shall be in thy mouth sweet as honey." How true it is that the words of Jesus are "sweet as honey," but when we digest them, assimilate them, and make them a vital part of us, they can bring about some very testing and trying experiences. Can you think of anything sweeter or more beautiful than these words in the Sermon òn the Mount; ". . . resist not evil: but whosoever shall smite thee on thy right cheek, turn to him the other also. And if any man will sue thee at the law, and take away thy coat, let him have thy cloak also. And whosoever shall compel thee to go a mile, go with him twain. Give to him that asketh thee, and from him that would borrow of thee turn not thou away. Ye have heard that it hath been said, Thou shalt love thy neighbour, and hate thine enemy. But I say unto you, Love your enemies, bless them that curse you, do good to them that hate you, and pray for them which despitefully use you, and persecute you."

Every Christian loves these teachings of Jesus, but who has ever put them into full practice without enduring hardships and even bitterness? All of us have found that the Christian life is not a bed of roses. When we have tried to pray for someone who has used us despitefully, it has been most trying and difficult. Resentment has built up in us, and we have to pray for ourselves first and beg for strength and grace. When someone smites us on the right cheek, there is a furious struggle inside of us. When someone pushes us or forces us to go a mile, there is always a bitter struggle before we can go the second mile. When someone sues us at the law or *takes* something that belongs to us, we spend a long time on our knees before we can *give* them something else that we cherish. Anyone who takes that little book and eats it and makes it a rule of life and a controlling influence is going to find it "sweet as honey" but bitter as wormwood. This is indeed a challenging picture that dares us to put one foot on the sea and one on the land and take that little book in our hands, keep it open in front of us and let it guide our lives.

Second, let us consider the importance of the material. The very fact that the angel stood with one foot on the earth makes us realize afresh that we must take cognizance of the material. I am afraid that oftentimes we preachers forget, in our enthusiasm to preach the importance of the spiritual, that God made this earth and that it is wholesome and precious and valuable. God expects us to build our homes, toil unceasingly, pay our debts, pay our life insurance, and meet our worldly obligations. I think this is one reason why God created such a beautiful world. He hid in this good earth all the things that we would need to build a comfortable and delightful civilization. Then he gave us the ingenuity necessary to think his thoughts and track his mind. Some of the things he hid from us so that we could only find them when we were ready spiritually to use them. Several recent writers have boldly stated that we are ahead of schedule in the discovery of such things as atomic power. They turned with frightened minds to beg their fellow men to catch up spiritually and keep the balance of life, or otherwise the result may be chaos. I am startled at the up-to-dateness of this picture. If we lose the balance we are indeed lost.

Immediately this brings to mind the warning that Jesus pointed out in his teaching, the warning against standing too heavily on that left foot and the material things of life. One day a man came running to him asking, "What shall I do to inherit eternal life?" Jesus looked at him and loved him. He was a ruler; he was rich; he was young. He told him to obey the commandments.

He answered, "All these I have done from my youth up."

Jesus said to him, "Sell all thou hast and distribute unto the poor . . . and come, follow me." And you remember he went away sorrowfully because he was standing too heavily on his left foot.

A man rode out into his bountiful farm, looked at the crops—bumper crops, big crops—and in effect said to himself, "My barns won't hold this stuff. What am I going to do? I know what I'll do. I'll tear them down and build a big barn. I'll say to my soul, 'eat, drink and be merry, thou hast much goods laid up in store for you.' "

God said to him, "Thou fool. Your soul can't live on things like this, and this night, because you don't know how to feed it, it will be required of you." Now, I think this same thought was in Jesus' mind when they came to tempt him, and one of them said, "Is it lawful to give tribute unto Caesar?"

He said, "Show me tribute money." The man handed him a coin, and he said, "Whose is this image?"

"Caesar's."

Then he said, "Render therefore unto Caesar the things which are Caesar's; and unto God the things that are God's." Both are important, both the material and the spiritual.

Dr. W. D. Nowlin, one of the veteran preachers of

Florida, told me an incident from his life which splendidly illustrates this. He said, "A fine young man, whose name was John, was superintendent of the Sunday school in one of my churches. He had the esteem and confidence of the whole town, and when he opened his own business, it prospered immediately. John was a splendid Christian and never missed a service. He was active in every department of the church. He was a consistent tither and one of the most faithful Christians in the church.

"His business succeeded so that he moved into larger quarters, and at the end of the second year he opened a branch store in the next town. In the meantime, his tithe grew until he was by far the largest giver in the church. At the end of four years he had opened six branch stores, and his tithe had grown to $100 a week, but there his contribution stopped. Along there somewhere he asked to be relieved of the superintendency of the Sunday school until he could get his business organized better. He also stopped coming to prayer meeting, and then we began to miss him at church on Sunday. When I went to see him, he told me that his business demanded so much of his time that often he spent the week ends in one of the other towns getting things organized and straightened out. Though his income grew larger, his contributions stayed at $100 a week.

"One day I went down to his office. I closed the door behind me as I went in. I said to him, 'John, I'm worried about you. You are missing church and apparently you are losing interest in the kingdom's work, and I am afraid you are not giving your tithe to the Lord any longer.'

"He said, 'Brother Nowlin, my tithe is too big, and I thought a hundred dollars a week was enough to give to the Lord's work. My business is so big I don't have as much time as I used to have.'

"I said, 'John, will you get down here on your knees and pray with me?'

"After we knelt, I began the prayer like this: 'Dear Lord, you have prospered John too much. You have given him too much business and too much success, and his tithe is too big to give to you, so dear Lord, please for John's sake and for the kingdom's work, burn down some of his stores. Let some of them fail; take some of the business away from him so he can be the same John we used to love and who used to work so faithfully for you.'

"I felt John tremble a little, and then he spoke out, 'Mr. Nowlin, let me take up from there.' His prayer was one that came from a contrite and humble heart. He asked God's forgiveness. He promised he would do it differently from now on. John came back and took his place as superintendent again and became once more the leading spirit in our church." Yes, there is danger of letting your life become unbalanced and putting too much weight on your left foot and not putting enough time to the reading of the little guide-book.

Third, let us heed the importance of the spiritual. I believe Dr. Rutledge was thinking clearly when he pointed out that the angel stood with his *right* foot on the sea. Certainly Jesus emphasized the priority of the spiritual. Once he said very plainly, "Seek ye first the kingdom of God and his righteousness." To be sure, there can be danger in putting too much weight on the right foot. People sometimes become fanatical about religion. Our papers recently carried an illustration of this. A mother and father were arrested and taken to court because they had neglected to have a physician when their little girl was badly burned. At the time of the arrest, the wounds had not healed, and the child was in danger of losing her life. Ugly scars were on her face because no medical attention had been given to the burns. The defense of the parents in court was this: "We knew that God would heal her if he wanted her to live. If God didn't want her to live, the physicians couldn't possibly save her. God has cured people who were bitten by rattlesnakes, and God could heal her if he wanted to; so we left it to God, for we have deep faith in God."

All of us believe that God can do anything, but we must also believe that he expects us to make use of our minds and our common sense as well as the things he has put on the earth for our benefit. He expects us to live balanced lives. But the greatest danger is not of becoming fanatical or over-zealous in spiritual things. The greatest danger is that we shall neglect the spiritual.

An early story told by Norman Vincent Peale illustrates this thought beautifully. In substance he said, "I received a telephone call asking me to come to a home on Riverside Drive. As I stopped my car in the driveway and looked at the palatial mansion, I wondered what could trouble anyone who had a home like this. A butler ushered me into the spacious living room. Evidence of wealth was everywhere. Several choice paintings of old masters were on the walls. As I waited for the lady who had called me, I couldn't resist walking over to stand in front of one of the paintings. I was lost in its beauty when she entered and spoke. I apologized and added, 'Anyone that has the privilege of living in a room like this must be both deeply grateful and very happy.'

"Without a word, she walked over to a mahogany table in the center of the room and opened a drawer. She took out a pearl-handled revolver and laid it on the table and turned very slowly to face me. 'Dr. Peale, I would have used this on myself but for the embarrassment that it would have caused my friends and my loved ones. I am utterly miserable inside. Everything that you think is so attractive in this home is overshadowed by the misery that is in my heart.' "

Dr. Peale went on to say, "Material things alone were never intended to make life full and happy. You can be happy anywhere if your relationship with God is right, but you cannot be happy at all if your relationship with God is wrong."

And so the posture of the angel standing with one foot on the material and one foot on the spiritual and the guidebook in his hand is the picture that God wants us to keep in our minds that life may be full and abundant.

13

The Interrupted Sermon

z

And he preached the word unto them.
—Mark 2:2

The president of the seminary that I attended once said to all of us assembled in chapel, "Young men, when you get into the pastorate and someone asks you where he should start reading the Bible, tell him to start with the Gospel of Mark, because the very first chapters of the Gospel of Mark present the finest picture of the strong Son of God to be found anywhere in the world." This incident of the interrupted sermon is a vital part of the grand picture of the strong Son of God.

Jesus had been preaching and teaching and healing in the towns and villages not far from Capernaum. The whole country was in such an uproar that people were flocking to him from every quarter. They came in such crowds that he "could not openly enter in the city but was without in desert places." After a time he did enter Capernaum, and when it was noised that

118

he was in a certain house, the crowd gathered immediately. They packed the house and the yard to hear
Jesus preach.

Suddenly the sermon was interrupted by a thud of
falling mud and drifting thatch which dropped to the
floor in front of him. Of course, everybody's eyes went
to the ceiling. They saw a hole, and some men were
making the hole bigger. When it was large enough, the
men took off their sashes and tied them to the four
corners of a litter. Then they carefully lowered a man
down to the feet of Jesus. I imagine that the men lay on
their faces and looked down through the hole to see
what would happen. They had done all they could.
They had brought their friend to the feet of the Master.
They hadn't been able to get in the house; so they had
used the outside steps and had gone up on the flat
roof. Now they waited expectantly. Jesus looked on the
sick man and used a most endearing word and followed
it with a startling statement, "Son, thy sins be forgiven
thee." The crowd of church men and religious leaders
sitting around reacted instantly. I am sure indignation
and anger were written all over their faces. You can
almost see them nudge each other and shake their
heads in negation. They were thinking, "This man
blasphemes. Nobody but God can forgive sins. Anyhow, those men didn't bring him here to have his sins
forgiven. They brought him here to have him healed
of the palsy." Jesus listening with his mind heard what
their minds said and answered them audibly, "[Is] it
easier to say Thy sins be forgiven thee; or to say, Arise,
and walk? But that ye may know that the Son of man

hath power on earth to forgive sins, (then saith he to the sick of the palsy) Arise, take up thy bed, and go unto thine house." The man arose and took up his bed, and the sermon was over, and the preaching service was broken up. Everything was in turmoil and confusion, but it was a wonderful hour, and the story has many beautiful lessons in it. Let me point out three of them.

I have an idea that it would be very pleasing to God if one of our formal services was interrupted by four men who were so dead in earnest to have one man made whole spiritually that they couldn't wait till the sermon was over. I am thinking of an experience that Dwight L. Moody had. He said, "I was preaching in a revival one evening when a baby on the fourth bench in front of me suddenly cried out in a clear, strong voice. Then the mother was able to quiet it for a few minutes, and I preached along until it cried out again. When this had happened several times, everybody around that baby stopped looking at me, and with frowning faces they stirred nervously in their seats and looked at the mother, almost wondering out loud why she didn't take it outside instead of letting it disturb the whole service.

"I am sure God inspired me to stop preaching and say to them, 'I wish you people wouldn't pay any attention to that baby. It isn't bothering me. I can talk louder than any baby can cry, and you are embarrassing the little mother. Maybe she couldn't come to church except she bring the baby. Let's not worry about it any more.'

"I turned to the little mother and said, 'Are you a Christian, Mother?' She shook her head.

"I said to those people, 'There, she isn't a Christian, and she has come to church to hear the gospel. It seems to me—' I didn't get any further with what I was going to say. They were ahead of me. A dozen mothers were converging on that spot, every one of them reaching for that baby. They took it over to another room and took care of it.

"I forgot what I was preaching about, but it didn't matter. I said to them, 'This is what pleases God and will please God more than anything else in the world—that a dozen people would want to make it possible that one single unsaved person might have a chance to get forgiveness for sin.' It was one of those services that God just took over. I didn't need to preach another word. I talked on for a few minutes and gave an invitation. People crowded each other to accept it."

I think it would please God today if we wouldn't think of church and church services and sermons the way we do. I am sure there are many people who come up to the hour of worship with the thought that the church service is something that they will *endure* because it's the proper thing for them to do. It will be a grand day in the kingdom of God when people get so concerned over the spiritual lameness of others that four of them will go after one lost soul.

What a refreshing thing it would be to a minister if the thing that happened to Mr. Finney would happen to one of us. A Supreme Court Judge walked up to the platform where Mr. Finney was preaching and stopped him in the middle of his sermon to say, "I want to be a Christian *now*. I want to make my profession of faith, and I don't want to wait any longer." I wonder if we preachers of today lack the fervor of Moody and Finney and so are going to miss having a sermon interrupted by someone who wants the salvation that we have and want to offer to others.

Here is Jesus' own explanation of why some miracles were performed by him. There are no Sunday school teachers and preachers who haven't been asked the question, "Why don't we have miracles today like those in the New Testament?"

And most of us have answered, "We do have miracles today. Many of them more wonderful than those in the New Testament. To be sure, they are not the same kind of miracles. In Christ's own words the reason for the miracles of healing is plainly stated, 'That ye may know that the Son of man hath power on earth to forgive sins . . . I say to thee Arise.' " Isn't Jesus saying that these miracles were necessary to launch the kingdom, that they were necessary to convince people that he was really the Son of God, that they were necessary to persuade people that he had the power to forgive sins, that they were necessary to show his gentleness and compassion?

Now, beloved, far more miracles are performed today in the spiritual kingdom than those we read about in the New Testament. Let me illustrate. One year when Dr. Truett was on a world tour of missions, Dr. Ernest Thorne and I were doing our best to fill his preaching engagement at the Cowboy Encampment at Paisano, Texas. One afternoon, Ernest said something like this to me: "I was listening to you preach the other night and decided to tell you the most dramatic thing that ever happened to me at a church service. I was holding a revival in a schoolhouse at the foot of a mountain. The people had no church and no preacher, but some Christians in the neighborhood had asked me to come for a week and help them organize a church.

"On the third night of the meeting one of the men was waiting for me at the schoolhouse door. He was very excited when he spoke.

" 'Dr. Thorne, we've got trouble. Over by that tree is a group of men who have terrorized this whole country for a long time. They are all moonshiners, and they don't want a church here. They came down tonight to break up the meeting; so I guess this is the end of it.'

"I gathered the little group of Christians together, and we talked and prayed inside of the schoolhouse for a few minutes. I felt God with me as I walked over to the group under the trees and asked if their leader, calling him by name, was there.

"A man stood up and came over to me, and I said to him, smiling as I said it, 'Could I talk to you alone for a minute or two?'

"He answered, 'Sure.'

"We walked a little way from the group, and I quietly said to him, 'I understand you came down to break up the revival.'

"He nodded his head as he answered, 'That's right.'

" 'I want to make you a proposition,' I continued. 'I usually preach half an hour. It's about time to start the service. Won't you come on in the schoolhouse, all of you, and let me preach half of the sermon—fifteen minutes—and then I'll stop. If you still want to break up the meeting, you certainly can, for we can't stop you. There is nothing in the world that we can do, but I thought maybe you'd be a good sport and give me a chance.'

"The man stood there a minute or two, shifted from one foot to the other, and then said, 'Come on over and talk to the boys about that. Let's see what they say.'

"I went over, still smiling, and made my little speech to the boys. I said, 'There are sixteen or eighteen of you, and everybody is afraid of you. I guess you could do anything you wanted to do to me, but I still would like to preach one half of the sermon. Then I'll stop. Just don't hurt anybody. Tell us to get out, if you want to, and we'll adjourn.' They thought it over for a minute or two, and then took a vote. All were in favor, and they filed into the church.

"I walked up on the platform and told the congregation, 'Nothing is going to happen the first fifteen minutes of my sermon. Then I will stop, and that may be the end of the revival.'

Ernest said to me, "Roy, I never prayed so earnestly nor preached with such power as I did those first fifteen minutes. Then I stopped and held my watch up and said to the gang of men down in front of me, 'Well, that's half of it. What do you want me to do?' They looked at each other and shifted around a little, and then I said to them, 'I wish you would let me finish it. How many of you are willing for me to go on and finish the sermon? Put up your hands.' Every hand in the gang went up. Oh, how I preached after that!

"When the sermon was over, we bowed our heads in prayer. I said, 'If there are any of you people here tonight who would like to raise your hand and say to God, "I am not happy with my life. I would like to have my sins forgiven," would you just raise your hands now?' The leader of that gang put his hand up just as high as he could reach. A few of the others followed him.

"After the service was over that leader and four or five others sat down in the corner of the schoolhouse. The leader's question was this, 'Dr. Thorne, would God forgive a man who had killed another man?'

"I answered, 'Yes, God will forgive a man who has killed another man.'

"Earnestly he looked at me, 'Dr. Thorne, don't fool me. Tell me the truth. I have been sorry ever since I killed him.' He put his hands over his face and wept."

Then Ernest said, "Roy, the best revival service I ever had in my life I had right there."

To me that is the greater miracle that Jesus was talking about—far greater than the miracle of healing the man with the palsy—the miracle of healing a man of soul sickness.

God uses the interruptions of life just as Jesus used

this unusual one. Interruptions that come in our own lives are often opportunities for God to bless us in a special way, just as he blessed in Mr. Moody's sermon and Dr. Thorne's revival. I am sure that we often take the wrong attitude toward the upsets that come to us in life. We think of them as impostors. We are very much like the people who wanted Isaiah to "speak unto us smooth things," whereas the thing that we often need most is an interruption. Someone has said, "Interruptions are normal, just as change is normal, and we ought to look for the hand of God in life's severest disappointments."

Dr. J. Wallace Hamilton, in his book *Ride the Wild Horses* expresses it this way: "Look again at the interruptions of Jesus, even the minor ones. He didn't merely endure them; He employed them, and used every one of them to promote the purposes of God. When the man out of the crowd broke in on His teaching, He used the interruption to heighten His teaching. When the Pharisees broke in with their ugly criticism of His morals—eating, as they said, with publicans and sinners—He did not merely endure their criticism, He employed it; He took their nasty insinuations, which were meant to discredit Him, and made them the sounding board for the loveliest story in all literature—the story of the Prodigal Son. 'The Son of Man is come to seek and to save that which was lost.' Every interruption He accepted as a divine opportunity; every ugly thing He transformed into something beautiful. Even the Cross, which was the utmost interruption meant to destroy Him and His purpose forever, provided Him with a force by which He lifted men to the very heights of God."

I remember hearing a university president at Ridgecrest talking to the students about the life of Joseph. In substance he said, "We often think of Joseph as a great hero, and we are forever admiring the beautiful thing that he did for his brethren, his forgiveness, and his tolerant treatment of them. We forget so easily that Joseph was not always like that.

"In his boyhood days Joseph was a spoiled brat. Remember the morning he got up and told his brothers that he had had a dream last night and very arrogantly he told them that he saw all of them bow down and touch the ground in front of him and that he waved a wand above them and they all obeyed him. He seemed to think it was perfectly natural for him to be a ruler over them. Certainly his father coddled him, gave him a coat of many colors, never sent him into the field to tend the cattle or the horses. It is no wonder that his brethren were jealous of him, and it should not surprise us in the least that when they saw at a long distance this beautiful coat of many colors, so different from their sweat-stained clothes, that they decided they would do something about it. Their resentment was keen, and wrath and anger filled them completely. The answer was, 'Put him to death or sell him as a slave.'

"Look at him as he is in his boyhood days and as someone has well said, 'I cannot see a Prime Minister in him. There is nothing of the Secretary of State in his personality. But when I look at him a few years later after this shocking interruption of life has come to him and he is a steward in Potiphar's home, the makings of a Prime Minister are written all over him, and as he stands that day and looks at his brethren in Egypt he is a different man.' " What happened to bring about this change? One word will express it, the word *interruption*.

When some calamity befalls us and some disappointment or frustration breaks our hearts, when circumstances throw a roadblock before us, or when we run into a dead-end street or a blind alley, wouldn't it be well for us to look up? Maybe this is an occasion for a particular blessing from God. The day may come when our prayers will be filled with gratitude for this interruption.

14

A Glorious Church

That he might present it to himself a glorious church, not having spot, or wrinkle, or any such thing; but that it should be holy and without blemish.
—Ephesians 5:27

In the *Christian Herald* some years ago a traveling salesman related an interesting experience. It went about like this: "My firm sent me to a little village in the Cumberland Mountains about fifty miles from the railroad. I hired a man and a span of horses to drive me to it. As we came over a hill and looked down on the village, he stopped the horses and called my attention to the church that was set on a little knoll in the very center of the village, and then he said, 'That's the prettiest church I ever saw. Wait till you get down to it.' We rode in silence down the rough road. He stopped the buggy and I got out while he drove on to the livery stable. I stood a long time looking at that church. It was a dream of grace and beauty.

"The parsonage was next door, and I walked over and knocked. A tall mountaineer, rugged and strong, answered. I asked him if I could look at his church.

129

With a smile, he reached for his black felt hat, and we walked around to the front of the church.

"He said to me, 'Mister, we built this church ourselves. Nobody received a cent of pay. We gathered the stones from the mountains, cut the trees for the timber, and built it as a labor of love.'

"I repeated to him that it was a dream of grace and beauty.

"After a few minutes he spoke again. 'Mister, we learned a lot of valuable lessons when we built this church. Many of the rocks came out of the road. They were rocks that our buggies had bumped over and our horses stumbled over for years, but when we shaped them and polished them up a little, they became beautiful building stones for God's church.' He turned his face toward me and said, 'Do you get it?'

"I answered, 'Yes, I get it. The people we stumble over and bump against and who cause us unhappiness can be made beautiful building stones in the kingdom of God.'

"He seemed content for a little while and then he said, 'See that big rock over there against the cemetery fence? I had picked it out for a cornerstone. It was down in a deep ravine, but the colors in it made it look like agate. It took six of us and four mules a full day to get it out and up here. Our master mason came over to look at it, and he said, "Parson, it's a beauty. It will make the prettiest cornerstone in the world." Then he swung his hammer against it and the smile disappeared from his face. Again and again he tapped it, and then he said, "Parson, it has a flaw in it."

We poured buckets of water over it and washed the dirt and mud away and found the big flaw that ran through the center of it.'

"Again the mountaineer preacher looked at me and repeated his question, 'Do you get it?'

"And I answered him, 'Yes, I get it. Some of the most attractive personalities in the world, people who could become foundation stones in the kingdom of God, can't be used because they have a flaw in them.' "

When I finished reading the incident, I turned immediately to the fifth chapter of Ephesians and read what Paul said, "Christ also loved the church, and gave himself for it; that he might sanctify and cleanse it . . . that he might present it to himself a *glorious church*, not having spot, or wrinkle, or any such thing; but that it should be holy and without blemish." And the question immediately came to me, "What kind of a church would Jesus call a *glorious church?* What would be its ingredients; what would it be like?" Four things stood out above the others, and here they are:

First, a glorious church would need to have a *consecrated membership*. In Paul's description, he tells us that Christ gave himself that the people who belong to his church might be sanctified and cleansed. No church that isn't made up of consecrated Christian people will ever be glorious. If it doesn't have love for God as its center, it will be "as sounding brass or a tinkling cymbal." There no place in a glorious church for worldly people. They are like the stone with a flaw in it. God needs for his building stones purity of heart and full surrender.

Mr. James A. Kraft, of the Kraft Cheese Company, preached in our church just before he died. He closed his sermon with this incident from his own life—a story I have never forgotten.

"Just before I left Chicago to go to the West Coast on a business trip, a mother came up to my office. She told me that she had noticed in the papers that I was going to San Francisco. Then she choked up and couldn't talk for a moment. Between her sobs she told me that her boy was in Alcatraz for life, and she begged me to go to see him while I was in the West.

"The day came when I sat in the warden's office and talked to him about the boy. Then he said to me, 'Walk down that corridor, Mr. Kraft, and the guards will direct you to the visiting rooms.'

"The corridor was steel lined and very narrow. As I turned the first corner a big guard thrust his hand out in front of me and said, 'Stand still just a moment.' I heard a buzzer and dimly saw a flash of light, then his voice again, 'You may pass. You are clean.'

"A little indignantly I said, 'Of course, I'm clean. What do you mean?'

"He smiled as he answered, 'I just took a good look, with the help of the lights, to see what you had in your pockets, and I repeat, You are clean.'

"My curiosity was aroused, and I asked, 'What do I have in my pockets?'

"He said, 'In your right trousers pocket you have some change; in your left one you have your car keys;

a fountain pen with a gold band around it is in your inside pocket.'

"I smiled as I walked down the corridor, and then suddenly I stood stock-still, for the question had come to me, 'Suppose when I turned the next corner Jesus would stick out his hand and say, "Stand still, Mr. Kraft, I want to see if you are clean—*inside*." '

"My mind flashed back over my life, then I heard myself whisper, 'Master, am I clean inside?'

"Very humbly I say it, but it seemed to me my Father in heaven answered, 'This is my beloved son in whom I am well pleased.' " A glorious church will be made up of people who are clean inside. The word for it is consecration.

Second, a glorious church will have a glorious *prayer life*. Five times I heard Dr. Truett preach on intercessory prayer. The great-souled preacher, who in many ways surpassed us all, had a strong conviction that a man could not be much of a Christian without praying for others. He believed it so firmly that even his morning prayers in the pulpit—prayers that were sometimes almost breath-taking, were for others. I have a number of letters from him and in each one of them he stirred my very soul by saying, "I pray for you continually," or "I always remember you by name in my prayers." If there was a secret to his greatness, I believe it was his prayer life, and I believe that a great part of it was his intercessory prayer life. Prayer not only changes things, but it changes the *pray-er*.

Even as I wrote this paragraph, I was interrupted by a young minister who came to talk to me about trouble in his church. The church is on the verge of splitting in two. He finished his heartbreaking story with this sentence, "Our church is not a praying church. Our prayer meetings are changed into business conferences about every other week. If there was just some way to get them down on their knees, we could save a church for the kingdom."

Dr. Ilion Jones, a great Presbyterian preacher, told a group of us this interesting incident. In substance he said, "Stuart Chase spoke to our convention in New York recently and told an incident in the third person, but we were all sure that he was speaking of his own experience.

"He said, 'A young man had a good position in a bank. Promotion was in front of him. Everybody on the Board of Directors liked him. The president and the vice-president liked him. Then a proposition came to him. A position opened where he could make a million dollars in a few months. It bothered him. The proposition wasn't all good. There were some shady sides to it. One morning at the breakfast table, he told his mother about the whole situation and asked her what he should do.'

"He said, 'That fine old Scotch Christian mother of his sat perfectly still with her head bowed in prayer a long time, and then with her eyes sparkling she looked across the table at him and said, "My son, when I come to awake you in the morning, I shake you hard, and you don't stir. I shake you harder, and you moan a little. I shake you harder still, and you open one eye, and then I shake you hard sure enough, and you awaken. My son, I would hate to come some morning to awaken you and find you wide awake." '

"Stuart Chase continued, 'The boy didn't take the position. He was guided by his mother's prayer, and he still sleeps.' "

Third, a glorious church will be a church with a glorious *missionary zeal*. No church that isn't interested and actively at work in sending the gospel story to other people has a right to exist. Dr. Maddry stressed this one day as he spoke at Ridgecrest and told the following impressive incident. He said, "One day a deacon took me in his buggy to a beautiful section of the country in North Carolina. As we came around a bend in the road, we came face to face with the most dilapidated church I had ever seen. It was sway-backed, and some of the shingles were missing from the roof; the shutters sagged on their hinges; the steps were broken; the paint was gone; the fence was half down, and the gate leaned on one hinge. The yard was grown up as high as your head with weeds. It was a miserable sight. I was half afraid to ask my friend what kind of a church it was. I was afraid he might say 'Baptist,' and that's exactly what he did say.

"I blurted out, 'Why don't you burn it down? It's a disgrace!'

"He answered with a smile, 'You don't understand, Doctor. That church preaches us a sermon every day. We wouldn't burn it down for anything. You never preached a missionary sermon in your life as powerful as the sermons that church preaches. Just sit still a minute and then you will understand.'

"We drove around a few more bends and then came face to face with one of the most beautiful country churches I have ever seen. Its lawns were well kept; its fences were whitewashed; the shutters were green; flowers bloomed around the whole front. It was a dream. Once more I was afraid to ask him what kind of a church it was. I was afraid he *wouldn't* say 'Baptist.'

"Then he spoke. 'This is our Baptist Church, and here's the reason we won't burn the other one down. We all worshiped in the old dilapidated church until we got a new preacher, and he began to preach missions. His heart was on fire to send the gospel to the dark lands of the world. About half of us caught some of his zeal, but the other half didn't want to be missionary. We had a meeting and decided we wouldn't have a church fuss. We agreed that the half of us that believed in missions would build another church and take the preacher with us, and we would give the old church to the others. This is the new church that we built, and one by one all of the others have come to join us. We agreed to let the old building stand as a witness to the great truth that missions are a part of Christ's plan, and the church that doesn't believe in missions has no reason to live.' " When Christ said, "Go ye into all the world," he wasn't talking just to twelve men, or to seventy, or to the Christians of Jerusalem. He was talking to us.

Fourth, a glorious church will have a glorious vision of *stewardship*. One of the best businessmen on the gold coast of Florida told me recently that he had learned a startling fact from the accounting firm that audited his

books each year. The representative said to him, "I
am glad to see your firm tithes, and I am glad that you
tithe personally, too." The businessman answered,
"Thank you. I guess you are a tither yourself?"

After a moment he said very slowly, "No, I never got
around to it, but I ought to, because I have been
auditing books in Miami for more than twenty years,
and I have never seen a firm that tithes go bankrupt
or even get in serious trouble." My friend said, "Say
that over again, for it interests me deeply." The
auditor took his glasses off and talked for ten minutes
naming some of the finest business firms in Florida that
were tithers.

Then I thought of what Warren Huyck said when I
asked him how many tithers were in his church, and
he answered, "Nineteen hundred." That startled me,
and I asked him how many members there were, and
he said, "Nineteen hundred." I exclaimed, "How in
the world did you ever get them all to tithe?"

His answer is a classic. "Only about one hundred
bring their tithes to the church. God collects it from
the rest of them." And he added, "I mean it, Dr.
Angell. God collects it from the rest of them." I sat
there with my mouth open wondering, wondering if it
were so, wondering if it were true, and I came to the
conclusion that Dr. Huyck was right. We can be *good*
stewards and bring our tithes to the church or we can
just be stewards and pay the collections when God
comes after them.

Beloved, your relationship to your possessions is one
of the most important elements in your spiritual life. It

is important for your peace of mind; it is important
for your relationship to God; it is important for
financing the kingdom; it is important for the joy that
you get out of Christianity. It is important for still
another thing. Read the third chapter of Malachi.
God said, "Prove me . . . if I will not open unto you
the windows of heaven, and pour you out a blessing
that there shall not be room enough to receive it."
Isn't he saying that our very prosperity depends upon
our accepting his plan?